My Children!
My Africa!

by Athol Fugard

A SAMUEL FRENCH ACTING EDITION

SAMUEL
FRENCH
FOUNDED 1830
New York Hollywood London Toronto
SAMUELFRENCH.COM

ISBN   978-0-573-69193-5   Printed in U.S.A.   · #15218

IMPORTANT BILLING AND CREDIT REQUIREMENTS

All producers of MY CHILDREN! MY AFRICA! *must* give credit to the Author of the Play in all programs distributed in connection with performances of the Play and in all instances in which the title of the Play appears for purposes of advertising, publicizing or otherwise exploiting the Play and/or a production. The name of the Author *must* also appear on a separate line, on which no other name appears, immediately following the title, and *must* appear in size of type not less than fifty percent the size of the title type.

The following credit must also appear in all programs :

"Originally produced by The Market Theatre,
Johanesburg, June, 1989.
"Originally produced in New York by The New York Theatre
Workshop"

For LISA and JOHN

My Chidlren! My Africa! was originally produced by The Market Theatre, Johannesburg, and subsequently made its American premiere at the The New York Theatre Workshop in December 1989, under the direction of Athol Fugard, with set and costume design by Susan Hilferty; lighting design by Dennis Parichy; sound design by Mark Bennett; and production stage management by Mary Michele Miner; with the following cast:

Mr. M..John Kani
ISABEL DYSON.......................Lisa Fugard
THAMI MBIKWANA........ Courtney B. Vance

CHARACTERS

Anela Myalatya (Mr. M)
Isabel Dyson
Thami Mbikwana

PLACE

Camdebo, South Africa

TIME

Autumn 1985.

ACT I

Scene 1

SCENE: Classroom of the Zolile High School.

AT RISE: MR. M is at a table with THAMI and ISABEL on either side of him. A lively inter-school debate is in progress. EVERYBODY is speaking at the same time.

MR. M. Order please!

ISABEL. I never said anything of the kind.

THAMI. Yes, you did. You said that women were more...

MR. M. I call you both to order!

ISABEL. What I said was that women ...

THAMI. ... were more emotional than men ...

ISABEL. Correction! That women were more intuitive than men ...

MR. M. Miss Dyson and Mr. Mbikwana! Will you both please ...

ISABEL. You are twisting my words and misquoting me.

THAMI. I am not. I am simply asking you ...

MR. M. Come to order! (*Grabs the school bell and rings it violently. It works. Silence.*) I think it is necessary for me to remind all of you exactly what a debate is supposed to be. (*Opens and reads from a little black dictionary that is at hand on the table.*) My dictionary defines it as follows: "the orderly and regulated discussion of an issue with opposing viewpoints receiving equal time and consideration." Shouting down the opposition so that they cannot be heard does not comply with that definition. Enthusiasm for your cause is most commendable but without personal discipline it is as useless as having a good donkey and a good cart but no harness. We are now running out of time. I am therefore closing the open section of our debate. No more interruptions from the floor please. We'll bring our proceedings to a close with a brief, I repeat *brief*, three minutes at the most, summing up of our arguments. Starting with the proposers of the motion: Mr. Thami Mbikwana of the Zolile High School, will you please make your concluding statement?

(*THAMI stands up. Wild round of APPLAUSE from the audience. HE is secure and at ease ... He is speaking to an audience of schoolmates. His "concluding statement" is outrageous and He knows it and enjoys it.*)

THAMI. I don't stand here now and speak to you as your friend and schoolmate. That would lessen the seriousness of my final words to you. No! Close your eyes, forget that you know my face and voice, forget that you know anything about Thami Mbikwana. Think of me rather as an oracle, of my words as those of the great ancestors of our traditional African culture, which we turn our back on and desert to our great peril!

The opposition has spoken about sexual exploitation and the need for women's liberation. Brothers and sisters these are foreign ideas. Do not listen to them. They come from a culture, the so-called Western Civilization, that has meant only misery to Africa and its people. It is the same culture that shipped away thousands of our ancestors as slaves, the same culture that has exploited Africa with the greed of a vulture during the period of Colonialism and the same culture which continues to exploit us in the twentieth century under the disguise of concern for our future.

The opposition has not been able to refute my claim that women cannot do the same jobs as men because they are not the equals of us physically and that a woman's role in the family, in society is totally different to that of a man's. These facts taken together reinforce what our fathers, and our grandfathers and our great Grandfathers knew; namely that happiness and prosperity for the tribe and the nation is achieved when education of the little ladies takes these facts into consideration. Would it be right for a woman to go to war while man sits at the sewing machine? I do not have milk in my breasts to feed the baby while my wife is out digging up roads for the Divisional Council. (*Wild laughter.*)

Brothers and sisters, it is obvious that you feel the same as I do about this most serious matter. I hope that at the end of this debate, your vote will reflect your agreement with me. (*Wild APPLAUSE and WHISTLES.*)

MR. M. Thank you Mr. Mbikwana.

(*THAMI sits.*)

MR. M. And now finally, a last statement from the captain of the visiting team, Miss Isabel Dyson of Camdeboo Girls high.

ISABEL. (*Polite APPLAUSE. Stands. SHE takes on the audience with direct unflinching eye contact. SHE is determined not to be intimidated.*) You have had to listen to a lot of talk this afternoon about traditional values, traditional society, your great ancestors, your glorious past. In spite of what has been implied I want to start off by telling you that I have as much respect and admiration for your history and tradition as anybody else. I believe most strongly that there are values and principles in traditional African society which could be studied with great profit by the Western Civilization so scornfully rejected by the previous speaker. But at the same time, I know, and you know, that Africa no longer lives in that past. For better or for worse it is part now of the twentieth century and all the nations on this continent are struggling very hard to come to terms with that reality. Arguments about sacred traditional values, the traditional way of life et cetera and et cetera, are used by those who would like to hold back Africa's progress and keep it locked up in the past.

Maybe there was a time in the past when a woman's life consisted of bearing children and hoeing the fields while men sharpened their spears and sat around waiting for another war to start. But it is a silly argument that relies on that old image of primitive Africa for its strength. It is an argument that insults your intelligence. Times have changed. Sheer brute strength is not the determining factor anymore. You do not need the muscles of a prize fighter when you sit down to operate the computers that control today's world. The American space program now has women astronauts on board the space shuttle doing the same jobs as men. As for the difference in the emotional and intellectual qualities of men and women, remember that it is a question of difference and not inferiority, and that with those differences go strengths which compensate for weaknesses in the opposite sex.

And lastly, a word of warning. The argument against equality for women, in education or any other field, based on alleged "differences" between the two sexes, is an argument that can very easily be used against any other "different" group. It is an argument based on prejudice, not fact. I ask you not to give it your support. Thank you. (*SHE sits. Polite APPLAUSE.*)

MR. M. Thank you Miss Dyson. We come now to the vote. But before we do that, a word of caution. We have had a wonderful experience this afternoon. Don't let it end on a frivolous and irresponsible note. Serious issues have

been debated. Vote accordingly. To borrow a phrase from
Mr. Mbikwana, forget the faces, remember the words. If
you believe that we have the right to vote out there in the
big world, then show here in the classroom that you know
how to use it. We'll take it on a count of hands, and for the
benefit of any over-enthusiastic supporters, only one hand
per person please. Let me read the proposal once again:
"That in view of the essential physical and psychological
differences between men and women, there should be
correspondingly different educational syllabuses for the two
sexes." All those in favor raise a hand.

(MR. M, THAMI and ISABEL count hands.)

MR. M. Seventeen?

(THAMI and ISABEL nod agreement.)

MR. M. All those against.

(THEY all count again.)

MR. M. Twenty-four?

(Reactions from THAMI and ISABEL.)

MR. M. The proposal is defeated by twenty-four votes
to seventeen. Before we break, just a reminder about the
special choir practice this afternoon. Members of the choir
must please join Mrs. Magada in Number Two Classroom
after school. *(To Isabel and Thami.)* Allow me to offer you
my congratulations, Miss Dyson, on a most well deserved
victory. Would do you say, Mbikwana?
THAMI. *(To Isabel.)* Your concluding statement was a
knockout.

MR. M. You didn't do too badly yourself.
ISABEL. You made me so angry!
THAMI. (*All innocence.*) I did?
ISABEL. Ja, you did.

(*THAMI laughs.*)

ISABEL. I was beginning to think you actually believed what you were saying.
THAMI. But I do!
ISABEL. Oh, come on ...!
MR. M. (*Rubbing his hands with pleasure.*) All I can say is ... Splendid! Splendid! Splendid! The intellect in action. Challenge and response. That is what a good debate is all about. And whatever you do, young lady, don't underestimate your achievement in winning the popular vote. It wasn't easy for that audience to vote against Mbikwana. He's one of them, and a very popular "one of them," I might add. (*Waving a finger at Thami.*) You were quite shameless in the way you tried to exploit that loyalty.
THAMI. (*Another laugh.*) Was that wrong?
MR. M. No. As the saying goes, all is fair in love, war and debating. But the fact that you didn't succeed is what makes me really happy. I am very proud of our audience. In my humble opinion they are the real winners this afternoon. You two just had to talk and argue. Anybody can do that. They had to listen ... intelligently!
ISABEL. They certainly gave me a good time.
MR. M. That was very apparent, if I may say so, Miss Dyson. I can't thank you enough for coming to us today. I sincerely hope there'll be another occasion.
ISABEL. Same here.

MR. M. Good! (*Consults his watch.*) Now you must excuse me. There is a staff meeting waiting for me. Will you look after Miss Dyson please, Mbikwana?

THAMI. Yes, teacher.

(*MR. M leaves. ISABEL and THAMI pack away into their school cases the papers and books they used in the debate. Without the mediating presence of Mr. M THEY are both a little self-conscious. First moves in the ensuing conversation are awkward.*)

ISABEL. I wish we had a teacher like ... Mr. ...(*Pronouncing the name carefully.*) ... M ya lat ya. Did I say it right?

THAMI. Yes, you did, but nobody calls him that. He's just plain Mr. M to everybody.

ISABEL. Mr. M.

THAMI. That's right.

ISABEL. Well, I think he's wonderful.

THAMI. He's okay.

ISABEL. I had a geography teacher in standard seven who was a little bit like him. Full of fun and lots of energy.

THAMI. Ja, that's Mr. M all right. (*Pause.*)

ISABEL. I meant what I said to him. I really did have a good time.

THAMI. Same here.

ISABEL. You did? Because to be honest with you, I wasn't expecting it.

THAMI. Me neither.

ISABEL. No?

THAMI. Nope.

ISABEL. Why not?

THAMI. (*Embarrassed.*) Well ... you know ...

ISABEL. Let me guess. You've never debated with girls before.

(*HE nods, smiling sheepishly.*)

ISABEL. And white girls at that! I don't believe it. You boys are all the same.

THAMI. But you were good!

ISABEL. Because I happen to feel very strongly about what we were debating. But it was also the whole atmosphere, you know. It was so ... so free and easy. The debates at my school are such stuffy affairs. And so boring most of the time. Everything is done according to the rules with everybody being polite and nobody getting exited ... lots of discipline but very little enthusiasm. This one was a riot!

THAMI. (*Finger to lips.*) Be careful.

ISABEL. Of what?

THAMI. That word.

ISABEL. Which one?

THAMI. Riot! Don't say it in a black township. Police start shooting as soon as they hear it.

ISABEL. Oh. I'm sorry.

THAMI. (*Having a good laugh.*) It's a joke, Isabel.

ISABEL. Oh ... you caught me off guard. I didn't think you would joke about those things.

THAMI. Riots and police? Oh yes, we joke about them. We joke about everything.

ISABEL. Okay, then I'll say it again; this afternoon was a riot.

THAMI. Good! Try that one on your folks when you get home tonight. Say the newspapers have got it all wrong. You had a wonderful time taking part in a little township riot.

(This time ISABEL does get the joke. A good laugh.)

ISABEL. Oh ja, I can just see my mom and dad cracking up at that one.

THAMI. They wouldn't think it was funny? *(The subject of white reaction to location humor amuses him enormously.)*

ISABEL. Are you kidding? They even take the Marx Brothers seriously. I can just hear my mom: "Isabel, I think it is very wrong to joke about those things."

THAMI. Dyson! That's an English name.

ISABEL. Sober, sensible, English-speaking South African. I'm the third generation.

THAMI. What does your dad do?

ISABEL. He's a chemist. The chemist shop in town. Karoo Pharmacy. That's ours. My mother and sister work in it as well, and on Saturdays, provided there isn't a hockey match; so do I.

THAMI. Any brothers?

ISABEL. No. Just the four of us.

THAMI. A happy family.

ISABEL. Ja, I suppose you could call us that. Mind you, Lucille would say it would be a lot happier if her little sister would be, as she puts it, "more accommodating of others."

THAMI. What does she mean?

ISABEL. She means she doesn't like the fact that I've got opinions of my own. I'm the rebel in the family.

THAMI. That sounds most interesting.

ISABEL. I can't help it. Whenever it's time for a family indaba ... you know, when we sit down in the lounge to discuss family business and things ... I just always seem to end up disagreeing with everybody and wanting to do things differently. But other than that, Ja, an average sort of family. What else do you want to know?

Go ahead, anything ... provided I also get a turn to ask questions.

(*THAMI studies her.*)

ISABEL. Eighteen years old. I think I want to be a writer. My favorite subject is English and my favorite sport, as you might have guessed, is hockey. Anything else?

THAMI. Yes. What did you have for breakfast this morning?

ISABEL. Auntie, our maid, put down in front of me a plate of steaming, delicious jungle oats over which I sprinkled a crust of golden, brown sugar, and while that was melting on top I added a little moat of chilled milk all around the side. That was followed by brown-bread toast, quince jam and lots and lots of tea.

THAMI. Yes, you're a writer.

ISABEL. You think so?

THAMI. You made me hungry.

ISABEL. My turn now?

THAMI. Yep.

ISABEL. Let's start with your family.

THAMI. Mbikwana!! (*HE clears his throat.*) Mbikwana is an old Bantu name and my mother and my father are good, reliable, ordinary, hardworking, Bantu-speaking, black South African natives. I am the one hundred thousandth generation.

ISABEL. You really like teasing, don't you.

THAMI. Amos and Lilian Mbikwana. They're in Cape Town. My mother is a domestic and my father works for the railways. I stay here with my grandmother and married sister. I was sent to school in the peaceful platteland because it is so much safer, you see, than the big city with

all its temptations and troubles. (*THAMI laughs.*) Another
Bantu joke.
    ISABEL. You're impossible!

(*THEY are now beginning to relax with each other.
ISABEL finds the class register on the desk.*)

    ISABEL. "Zolile High School. Standard Ten." (*SHE
opens it and reads.*) Awu.
    THAMI. (*Pointing to the appropriate desk in the
classroom.*) There. Johnny. Center-forward in our soccer
team.
    ISABEL. Bandla.
    THAMI. There.
    ISABEL. Cwati.
    THAMI. Cwati. There.
    ISABEL. Who was the chap sitting there who laughed
at *all* your jokes and applauded *everything* you said.
    THAMI. Stephen Gaika. He's mad!
    ISABEL. And your best friend?
    THAMI. They are all my friends.
    ISABEL. And where does ... (*SHE finds his name in
the register.*) ... Thami Mbikwana sit?

(*THAMI points. ISABEL goes to the desk and sits.*)

    THAMI. Yes, that's the one. For nearly two years I've
sat there ... being educated!
    ISABEL. (*Reading names carved into the wood of the
desk.*) John Bobby, Zola, Bo ... Boni ...
    THAMI. Bonisile.
    ISABEL. Where's your name?
    THAMI. You won't find it there. I don't want to leave
any part of me in this classroom.
    ISABEL. That sounds very heavy.

THAMI. It's been heavy. You've got no problems with it, hey.

ISABEL. With school? No, not really. Couple of teachers have tried their best to spoil it for me, but they haven't succeeded. I've had a pretty good time, in fact. I think I might even end up with the old cliche ... you know, school years, best years, happiest years ... Whatever it is they say.

THAMI. No. I won't be saying that.

ISABEL. That surprises me.

THAMI. Why?

ISABEL. Ja, come on, wouldn't you be if I said it? You're obviously clever. I'll bet you sail through your exams.

THAMI. It's not as simple as just passing exams, Isabel. School doesn't mean the same to us that it does to you.

ISABEL. Go on.

THAMI. I used to like it. Junior school? You should have seen me. I wanted to have school on Saturdays and Sundays as well. Yes, I did. Other boys wanted to kill me. I hated the holidays.

ISABEL. So what happened?

THAMI. I changed.

ISABEL. Ja, I'm listening.

THAMI. (*A shrug.*) That's all. I changed. Things changed. Everything changed.

ISABEL. (*Realizing she is not going to get any more out of him.*) Only five months to go.

THAMI. I'm counting.

ISABEL. What then?

THAMI. After school? (*Another shrug.*) I don't know yet. Do you?

ISABEL. Ja. Rhodes University. I want to study journalism.

THAMI. Newspaper reporter.

ISABEL. And radio, TV. It's a very wide field now. You can specialize in all sorts of things. (*Perplexed.*) Don't you want to study further, Thami?

THAMI. I told you. I'm not sure about anything yet.

ISABEL. What does Mr. M say?

THAMI. It's got nothing to do with him.

ISABEL. But you're his favorite, aren't you?

(*Non-committal shrug from THAMI.*)

ISABEL. I bet you are. And I also bet you anything you like that he's got a career planned out for you.

THAMI. (*Sharply.*) What I do with my life has got nothing to do with him.

ISABEL. Sorry.

THAMI. I don't listen to what he says and I don't do what he says.

ISABEL. I said I'm sorry, I didn't mean to interfere.

THAMI. That's all right. It's just that he makes me so mad sometimes. He always thinks *he* knows what is best for me. He never asks me how I feel about things. I know he means well, but I'm not a child anymore. I've got ideas of my own now.

ISABEL. (*Placating.*) Ja, I know what you mean. I've had them in my life as well. They always know what is best for you, don't they? So anyway, listen ... I'm going to write up the debate for our school newspaper. I'll send you a copy if you like.

THAMI. You got a school newspaper! How about that!

ISABEL. It's a bit unethical reporting on a contest in which I took part, and won, but I promise to be objective. I made notes of most of your main points.

THAMI. You can have my speech if you want it.

ISABEL. Hell, thanks. That will make it much easier ... and guarantee there won't be any misquotes!

(*THAMI hands over the speech. It is obvious that THEY both want to prolong the conversation, but this is prevented by the sound of Mr. M's BELL being rung vigorously in the distance. THEY check wristwatches.*)

ISABEL. Oh, my God, look at the time!

(*THEY grab their schoolcases and run.*)

Scene 2

ISABEL. (*Alone. SHE speaks directly to the audience.*) It's on the edge of town, on the right hand side when you drive out to join the National Road going north to Middleberg. Unfortunately, as most of Camdeboo would say, you can't miss it. I discovered the other day that it has actually got a name ... Brakwater ... from the old farm that used to be there. Now everybody just calls it "the location." There's been a lot of talk lately about moving it to where it can't be seen. Our mayor, Mr. Pienaar, was in our shop the other day and I heard him say to my dad that it was "very much to be regretted" that the first thing that greeted any visitor to the town was the "terrible mess of the location." To be fair to old Pienaar, he has got a point, you know. Our town is very pretty. We've got a lot of nicely restored National Monument houses and buildings. Specially in the Main Street. Our shop is one of them. The location is quite an eyesore by comparison. Most of the houses if you can call them that!—are made of bits of old corrugated iron or anything else they could find to make

four walls and a roof. There are no gardens or anything like
that. You've got to drive in first gear all the time because
of the potholes and stones, and when the wind is blowing
and all the dust and rubbish flying around ...! I think you'd
be inclined to agree with our mayor.

I've actually been into it quite a few times. With my
mom to visit Auntie, our maid, when she was sick. And
with my dad when he had to take emergency medicines to
the clinic. I can remember one visit, just sitting in the car
and staring out of the window trying to imagine what it
would be like to live my whole life in one of those little
pondoks. No electricity, no running water. No privacy!
Auntie's little house has only got two small rooms and
nine of them sleep there. I ended up being damn glad I was
born with a white skin.

But don't get the wrong idea. I'm not saying I've spent
a lot of time thinking about it seriously or anything like
that.

It's just been there, you know, on the edge of my life,
the way it is out there on the edge of town. So when Miss
Brockway, our principal, called me in and told me that the
black school had started a debating society and had invited
us over for a debate, I didn't have any objections. She said
it was a chance for a "pioneering intellectual exchange"
between the two schools.

She also said she had checked with the police and they
had said it would be all right, provided we were driven
straight to the school and then straight out afterwards.
There's been a bit of trouble in the location again and
people are starting to get nervous about it. So off we went
... myself, Renee Vermaas and Cathy Bullard, the C.G.H.
Debating Team ... feeling very virtuous about our
"pioneering" mission into the location. As Renee tactfully
put it: "Shame! We must remember that English isn't their

home language. So don't use too many big words and speak slowly and carefully."

They were waiting for us in what they called Number One Classroom. (*Shaking her head.*) Honestly, I would rate it as the most bleak, depressing, dingy classroom I have ever been in. Everything about it was grey—the cement floor, the walls, the ceiling.

When I first saw it I thought to myself, how in God's name does anybody study or learn anything in here? But there they were, about forty of them, my age, mostly boys, not one welcoming smile among the lot of them. And they *were* studying something and very intently ... three privileged and uncomfortable white girls, in smart uniforms, from a posh school, who had come to give them a lesson in debating. I know I'm a good debater and one of the reasons for that is that I always talk very directly to the audience and the opposition. I am not shy about making eye contact. Well, when I did it this time, when it was my turn to speak and I stood up and looked at those forty unsmiling faces, I suddenly realized that I hadn't prepared myself for one simple but all important fact: they had no intention of being grateful to me. They were sitting there waiting to judge me, what I said and how I said it, on the basis of total equality. Maybe it doesn't sound like such a big thing to you, but you must understand I had never really confronted that before, and I don't just mean in debates. I mean in my life!

I'm not saying I've had no contact across the color line. Good heavens no! I get as much of that as any average young white South African. I have a great time every morning with Auntie in the kitchen when she's cooking breakfast and we gossip about everything and everybody in town. And then there's Samuel with his crash helmet and scooter ... he delivers medicines for my dad ... I have wonderful long conversations with him about religion and the meaning of life generally. He's a very staunch Zionist. Church every Sunday. But it's always "Miss Isabel," the baas' daughter, that he's talking to. When I stood up in front of those black matric pupils in Number One classroom it was a very different story. I wasn't at home or in my dad's shop or in my school or any of the other safe places in my life.

I was in Brakwater! It was *their* school. It was *their* world. I was the outsider and I was being asked to prove myself. Standing there in front of them like that I felt ...exposed! ... in a way that has never happened to me before. Cathy told me afterwards that she's never heard me start a debate *so* badly and finish it *so* strongly.

God, it was good! I don't know when exactly it happened, but about halfway through my opening address, I realized that everything about that moment ... the miserable little classroom, myself, my voice, what I was saying and them hearing and understanding me, because I knew they understood me ... they were staring and listening so hard I could feel it on my skin! ... all of it had become one of the most real experiences I have ever had. I have never before had so ... so exciting! ... a sense of myself. Because that *is* what we all want, isn't it? For things to be real, our lives, our thoughts, what we say and do? That's what I want, now. I didn't really know it before that debate, but I do now. You see, I finally worked out what happened to me in the classroom. I discovered a new world! I've always thought about the location as just a sort of embarrassing backyard to our neat and proper little white world, where our maids and our gardeners and our delivery boys went at the end of the day. But it's not. It's a whole world of its own with its own life that has nothing to do with us. If you put together all the Brakwaters in the country, then it's a pretty big one ... and if you'll excuse my language .. .there's a hell of a lot of people living in it! That's quite a discovery you know. But it's also a little ... what's the word? ... disconcerting! You see, it means that what I thought was out there for me ... No, it's worse than that! It's what I was made to believe was out there for me ... the ideas, the chances, the people ... 'specially the people! ...all of that is only a small fraction of what it could be. (*Shaking her head.*) No. Or as Auntie says in the kitchen, when she's not happy about something ... Aikona! Not good enough. I'm greedy. I want more. I want as much as I can get.

Scene 3

AT RISE: ISABEL alone.

MR. M enters, hat in hand, mopping his brow with a handkerchief.

MR. M. Miss Dyson! There you are.

ISABEL. (*Surprised.*) Hello!

MR. M. My apologies for descending on you out of the blue like this, but I've been looking for you high and low. One of your schoolmates said I would find you here.

ISABEL. Don't apologize. It's a pleasure to see you again, Mr. M.

MR. M. (*Delighted.*) Mr. M! How wonderful to hear you call me that.

ISABEL. You must blame Thami for my familiarity.

MR. M. Blame him? On the contrary, I will thank him most gratefully. Hearing you call me Mr. M like all the others at the school gives me a happy feeling that you are also a member of my very extended family.

ISABEL. I'd like to be.

MR. M. Then welcome to my family, Miss—

ISABEL. (*Beforehe can say it.*) "Isabel" if you please Mr. M, just plain Isabel.

MR. M. (*Bowing.*) Then doubly welcome, young Isabel.

ISABEL. (*Curtsy.*) I thank you kind sir.

MR. M. You have great charm, young lady. I can understand now how you managed to leave so many friends behind you after only one visit to the school. Hardly a day passes without someone stopping me and asking: When is Isabel Dyson and her team coming back?

ISABEL. Well? When are we?

MR. M. You would still welcome a return visit?

ISABEL. But of course.

MR. M. Why so emphatically "of course?"

ISABEL. Because I enjoyed the first one so emphatically very much.

MR. M. The unruly behavior of my young family wasn't too much for you?

ISABEL. Didn't I also get a little unruly once or twice, Mr. M?

MR. M. Yes, now that you mention it. You certainly gave as good as you got.

ISABEL. (*With relish.*) And that is precisely why I enjoyed myself ...

MR. M. You like a good fight.

ISABEL. Ja. 'Specially the ones I win!

MR. M. Splendid! Splendid! Splendid! Because that is precisely what I have come to offer you.

ISABEL. Your Thami wants a return bout, does he?

MR. M. He will certainly welcome the opportunity to salvage his pride when it comes along ... his friends are teasing him mercilessly ... but what I have come to talk to you about is a prospect even more exciting than that. I have just seen Miss Brockway and she has given it her official blessing. It was her suggestion that I approach you directly. So here I am. Can you spare a few minutes?

ISABEL. As many as you like.

MR. M. It came to me as I sat there in Number One trying to be an impartial referee, while you and Thami went for each other hammer and tongs, no holes barred and no quarter given or asked. I don't blame our audience for being so unruly. Once or twice I felt like doing some shouting myself. What a contest! But at the same time, what a waste, I thought! Yes, you heard me correctly. A waste! They shouldn't be fighting each other. They should be fighting together! If the sight of them as opponents is so exciting, imagine what it would be like if they were allies. If those two stood side by side and joined forces, they could take on anybody ... and win! For the next few days that is all I could think of. It tormented me. When I wrote my report about the debate in the school diary, that was the last sentence. "But , oh what a waste!"

The truth is, I've seen too much of it, Isabel. Wasted people! Wasted chances! It's become a phobia with me now. It's not easy, you know, to be a teacher, to put your heart and soul into educating an eager young mind which you know will never get a chance to develop further and realize its full potential. The thought that you and Thami would be another two victims of this country's lunacy, was almost too much for me.

The time for lamentations is passed. (*Envelope from his pocket.*) Two days ago I received this in the mail. It's the program for this year's Grahamstown Schools Festival. It has given me what I was looking for ... an opportunity to fight the lunacy. The Standard Bank is sponsoring a new event: An inter-school English literature quiz. Each team to consist of two members. I'll come straight to the point. I have suggested to Miss Brockway that Zolile High and Camdeboo High join forces and enter a combined team. As

I have already told you, she has agreed and so has the Festival director who I spoke to on the telephone this morning. There you have it, Isabel Dyson. I anxiously await your response.

ISABEL. I'm on the team?

MR. M. Yes.

ISABEL. And ...? (*Her eyes brighten with anticipation.*)

MR. M. That's right.

ISABEL. Thami!

MR. M. Correct!

ISABEL. Mr. M, you're a genius!

MR. M. (*Holding up a hand to stop what was obviously going to be a very enthusiastic response.*) Wait! Wait! Before you get carried away and say yes, let me warn you about a few things. It's going to mean a lot of very hard work. I am appointing myself team coach and as Thami will tell you, I can be a very hard taskmaster. You'll have to give up a lot of free time, young lady.

ISABEL. Anything else?

MR. M. Not for the moment.

ISABEL. Then I'll say it again. Mr. M, you're a genius! (*Her joy is enormous and SHE shows it.*) How's that for unruly behavior?

MR. M. The very worst! They couldn't do it better on the location streets. What a heartwarming response, Isabel!

ISABEL. What were you expecting? That I would say no?

MR. M. I didn't know what to expect. I knew that you would give me a sympathetic hearing, but that I would be swept off my feet, literally and figuratively ... No. I was most certainly not prepared for that. Does my silly little idea really mean that much to you?

ISABEL. None of that, Mr. M! It's not silly and it's not little and you know it.

MR. M. All right. But does it really mean that much to you?

ISABEL. Yes, it does.

MR. M. (*Persistent.*) But why?

ISABEL. That visit to Zolile was one of the best things that has happened to me. I don't want it to just end there. One visit and that's it.

(*MR. M listens quietly, attentively, an invitation to Isabel to say more.*)

ISABEL. It feels like it could be the beginning of something. I've met you and Thami and all the others and I would like to get to know you all better. But how do I do that? I can't just go after you chaps like ... well, you know what I mean. Roll up and knock on your doors like you were neighbors or just living down the street. It's not as easy as that with us, is it? You're in the location, I'm in the town ... and all the rest of it. So there I was feeling more and more frustrated about it all when along you come with your "silly little" idea. It's perfect! Do I make sense?

MR. M. Most definitely. Make some more.

ISABEL. I've been thinking about it, you see. When I told my mom and dad about the debate and what a good time I'd had, I could see that they didn't really understand what I was talking about. 'Specially my mom. I ended up getting very impatient with her, which wasn't very smart of me because the harder I tried to make her understand the more nervous she got. Anyway, I've cooled off now and I realize why she was like that. Being with black people on an equal footing, you know ... as equals, because that is how I ended up feeling with Thami and his friends ... that was something that had never happened to her. She didn't know what I was talking about. And because she knows nothing about it, she's frightened of it.

MR. M. You are not.

ISABEL. No. Not anymore.

MR. M. So you were.

ISABEL. Well, not so much frightened as sort of uncertain. You see I thought I knew what to expect, but after a few minutes in Number One Classroom I realized I was wrong by a mile.

MR. M. What had you expected, Isabel?

ISABEL. You know, that everybody would be nice and polite and very, very grateful.

MR. M. And we weren't?

ISABEL. You were, but not them. Thami and his friends. (*SHE laughs at the memory.*) Ja, to be honest Mr. M, that family of yours *was* a bit scary at first. But not anymore! I feel I've made friends with Thami ... and the others, so now it's different.

MR. M. Simple as that.

ISABEL. Simple as that.

MR. M. Knowledge has banished fear.

ISABEL. That's right.

MR. M. Bravo. Bravo. And yet again Bravo! If you knew what it meant to me to hear you speak like that. I wasn't wrong. From the moment I first shook hands with you I knew you were a kindred spirit.

ISABEL. Tell me more about the competition.

MR. M. First prize is five thousand Rand which the Bank has stipulated must be spent on books for the school library. We will obviously divide it equally between Camdeboo and Zolile when you and Thami win.

ISABEL. Yes; what about my teammate. What does he say? Have you asked him yet?

MR. M. No, I haven't *asked* him Isabel, and I won't. I will *tell* him, and when I do I trust he will express as much enthusiasm for the idea as you have. I am an old fashioned traditionalist in most things, young lady, and my

classroom is certainly no exception. I teach, Thami learns.
He understands and accepts that that is the way it should
be. You don't like the sound of that do you?

ISABEL. Does sound a bit dictatorial, you know.

MR. M. It might sound that way, but I assure you it
isn't. We do not blur the difference between the generations
in the way that you white people do. Respect for authority,
right authority, is deeply ingrained in the African soul. It's
all I've got when I stand in there in Number One. Respect
for my authority is my only teaching aid. If I ever lost it
those young people will abandon their desks and take to the
streets. I expect Thami to trust my judgment of what is
best for him, and he does. That trust is the most sacred
responsibility in my life.

ISABEL. He's your favorite, isn't he?

MR. M. Good heavens! A good teacher doesn't have
favorites! Are you suggesting that I might be a bad one?
Because if you are .... (*Looking around.*) you would be
right, young lady. Measured by that yardstick I am a very
bad teacher indeed. He is my favorite. Thami Mbikwana!
Yes, I have waited a long time for him. To tell you the
truth I had given up all hope of him ever coming along.
Any teacher who takes his calling seriously, dreams about
that one special pupil, that one eager and gifted young head
into which he can pour all that he knows and loves and
who will justify all the years of frustration in the
classroom. There have been pupils that I'm proud of, but
I've always had to bully them into doing their school
work. Not with Thami. *He* wants to learn the way other
boys want to run out of the classroom and make mischief.
If he looks after himself he'll go far and do big things.
He's a born leader, Isabel, and that is what your generation
needs. Powerful forces are fighting for the souls of you
young people. You need *real* leaders. Not rabble-rousers. I
know Thami is meant to be one. I know it with such

certainty it makes me frightened. Because it is a responsibility. Mine and mine alone.

I've got a small confession to make. In addition to everything I've already said, there's another reason for this idea of mine. When you and Thami shine at the Festival, as I know you will, and win first prize and we've pocketed a nice little check for five thousand Rand, I am going to point to Thami and say: And now, ladies and gentlemen, a full university scholarship, if you please.

ISABEL. And you'll get it. We'll shine, we'll win, we'll pocket that check and Thami will get a scholarship.

MR. M. (*His turn for an enthusiastic response. Embarrassment and laughter.*) Your unruly behavior is very infectious!

ISABEL. *My* unruly behavior? I like that! I caught that disease in the location, I'll have you know.

MR. M. The future is ours, Isabel. We'll show this stupid country how it is done.

ISABEL. When do we start?

MR. M. Next week. We need to plan our campaign very carefully.

ISABEL. I'll be ready.

Scene 4

MR. M. (*Alone. HE talks directly to the audience.*) "I am a man who in the eager pursuit of knowledge forgets his food and in the joy of its attainment forgets his sorrow, and who does not perceive that old age is coming on." (*HE shakes his head.*) No. As I'm sure you have already guessed, that is not me. My pursuit of knowledge is eager, but I do perceive, and only too clearly, that old age is coming on, and at the best of times I do a bad job of forgetting my sorrows. Those wonderful words come from the finest teacher I have ever had, that most wise of all the ancient philosophers ... Confucius! Yes. I am a Confucian. A black Confucian! There are not many of us. In fact I think there's a good chance that the only one in the country is talking to you at this moment.

I claim him as my teacher because I have read very carefully, and many times, and I will read it many times more, a little book I have about him, his life, his thoughts and utterances. Truly, they *are* wonderful words, my friends, wonderful, wonderful words! My classroom motto comes from its pages: "Learning undigested by thought is labor lost. Thought unassisted by learning is perilous!" But the words that challenge me most these days, is something he said towards the end of his life. At the age of seventy he turned to his pupils once day and said that he could do whatever his heart prompted, without transgressing what was right.

What do you say to that?

Think about it. *Anything* his heart prompted, *anything* that rose up as a spontaneous urge in his soul, *without* transgressing what was right!

What a heart, my friends! Aren't you envious of old Confucius? Wouldn't it be marvelous to have a heart you could trust like that? Imagine being able to wake up in the morning in your little room, yawn and stretch, scratch a few flea bites and then jump out of your bed and eat your bowl of mealie-pap and sour milk with a happy heart because you know that when you walk out into the world you will be free to obey and act out, with a clear conscience, all the promptings of your heart. No matter what you see out there on the battle grounds of location streets, and believe me, there are days now when my eyesight feels more like a curse than a blessing, no matter what stories of hardship and suffering you hear, or how bad the news you read in the newspaper, knowing that the whole truth, which can't be printed, is even worse ... in spite of all that, you need have no fear of your spontaneous urges, because in obeying them you will not transgress what is right.

(*Another shake of his head, another rueful smile.*) No, yet again. Not in this life, and most certainly not in this world when I find myself, will those wonderful words of Confucius be mine. Not even if I lived to be one hundred and seventy, will I end up with a calm, gentle Chinese heart like his. I wish I could. Believe me, I really wish I could. Because I am frightened of the one I've got. I don't get gentle promptings from it, my friends. I get heart attacks. When I walk out into those streets, and I see what is happening to my people, it jumps out and savages me like a wild beast. (*Thumping his chest with a clenched fist.*) I've got a whole zoo in here, a mad zoo of hungry animals ... and the keeper is frightened! All of them. Mad and savage!

Look at me! I'm sweating today. I've been sweating for a week. Why? Because one of those animals, the one called Hope, has broken loose and is looking for food. Don't be fooled by its gentle name. It is as dangerous as Hate and Despair would be if they ever managed to break out. You think I'm exaggerating? Pushing my metaphor a little too far? Then I'd like to put you inside a black skin and ask you to keep Hope alive, find food for it on these streets where our children, our loved and precious children go hungry and die of malnutrition. No, believe me, it is a dangerous animal for a black man to have prowling around in his heart. So how do I manage to keep mine alive, you ask? Friends, I am going to let you in on a terrible secret. That is why I am a teacher.

It is all part of a secret plan to keep alive this savage Hope of mine. The truth is that I am worse than Nero feeding Christians to the lions. I feed young people to my Hope. Every young body behind a school desk keeps it alive.

So you've been warned! If you see a hungry gleam in my eyes when I look at your children ... you know what it means. That is the monster that stands here before you. Full name: Anela Myalatya. Age: fifty-seven. Marital status: bachelor. Occupation: teacher. Address: The back room of the Reverend Mbopa's house next to the Anglican Church of St. Mark. It's a little on the small side. You know those big kitchen size boxes of matches they sell these days ... well if you imagine one of those as Number One Classroom at Zolile High, then the little match box you put in your pocket is my room at the Reverend Mbopa's. But I'm not complaining. It has got all I need ... a table and chair where I correct homework and prepare lessons, and a comfortable bed for a good night's insomnia and a reserved space for my chair in front of the television set in the Reverend Mbopa's lounge.

So there you have it. What I call my life rattles around in these two matchboxes ... the classroom and the back room. If you see me hurrying along the streets you can be reasonably certain that one of those two is my urgent destination. The people tease me. "Faster, Mr. M" they shout to me from their front door. "You'll be late." They think it's a funny joke. They don't know how close they are to a terrible truth ...

Yes! The clocks are ticking, my friends. History has got a strict timetable. If we're not careful we might be remembered as the country where everybody arrived too late.

Scene 5

Mr. M waiting. ISABEL hurries on, carrying hockey stick, togs and her school case. SHE is hot and exhausted.

ISABEL. Sorry, Mr. M, sorry. The game started late.
MR. M. I haven't been waiting long.

(ISABEL unburdens herself and collapses with a groan.)

MR. M. Did you win?
ISABEL. No. We played a team of friendly Afrikaans-speaking young Amazons from Jansenville and they licked us hollow. Four–one! It was brutal! God, they were fit. And fast. They ran circles around us on that hockey field. I felt so stupid. I kept saying to myself "It's only a game, Isabel. Relax! Enjoy it! Have a good time!" But no, there I was swearing under my breath at poor little Hilary Castle for being slow and not getting into position for my passes. *(Laughing at herself.)* You want to know something really terrible? A couple of times I actually wanted to go over and hit her with my hockey stick. Isn't that awful? It's no good, Mr. M, I've got to face it: I'm a bad loser. Got any advice for me?
MR. M. On how to be a good one?
ISABEL. Ja. How to lose graciously. With dignity. I mean it. I really wish I could.
MR. M. If I did have advice for you Isabel, I think I would be well advised to try it out on myself first ...
ISABEL. Why? You one as well?

(MR. M nods.)

ISABEL. I don't believe it.

MR. M. It's true, Isabel. I'm ashamed to say it but when I lose I also want to grab my hockey stick and hit somebody.

(A good laugh from Isabel.)

MR. M. Believe me, I can get very petty and mean if I'm not on the winning side. I suppose most bachelors end up like that. We get so used to having everything our own way that when something goes wrong ... So there's my advice to you. Get married! If what I've heard is true, holy matrimony is the best school of all for learning how to lose.

ISABEL. I don't think it's something you can learn. You've either got it or you haven't. Like Thami. Without even thinking about it I know *he's* a good loser.

MR. M. Maybe.

ISABEL. No. No maybes about it. He'd never grab his hockey stick and take it out on somebody else if he didn't win.

MR. M. You're right. I can't see him doing that. You've become good friends, haven't you?

ISABEL. The best. These past few weeks have been quite an education. I owe you a lot, you know. I think Thami would say the same ... if you would only give him the chance to do so.

MR. M. What do you mean by that remark, young lady?

ISABEL. You know what I mean by that remark, *Mr. Teacher!* It's called Freedom of Speech.

MR. M. I've given him plenty of freedom, within reasonable limits, but he never uses it.

ISABEL. Because you're *always* the teacher and he's *always* the pupil. Stop teaching him all the time, Mr. M.

Try just talking to him for a change ... you know, like a friend. I bet you in some ways I already know more about Thami than you.

MR. M. I don't deny that. In which case tell me, is he happy?

ISABEL. What do you mean? Happy with what? Us? The competition?

MR. M. Yes, and also his school work and ... everything else.

ISABEL. Why don't you ask him?

MR. M. Because all I'll get is another polite "Yes, teacher." I thought maybe he had said something to you about the way he really felt.

ISABEL. (*Shaking her head.*) The two of you! It's crazy! But ja, he's happy. At least I think he is. He's not a blabber-mouth like me, Mr. M. He doesn't give much away ... even when we talk about ourselves. I don't know what it was like in your time, but being eighteen years old today is a pretty complicated business as far as we're concerned. If you asked me if I was happy, I'd say yes, but that doesn't mean I haven't got any problems. I've got plenty and I'm sure it's the same with Thami.

MR. M. Thami has told you he's got problems?

ISABEL. Come on, Mr. M! We've all got problems. I've got problems, you've got problems, Thami's got problems.

MR. M. But did he say what they were?

ISABEL. You're fishing for something, Mr. M. What is it?

MR. M. Trouble, Isabel. I'm sorry to say it, but I'm fishing for trouble and I'm trying to catch it before it gets too big.

ISABEL. Thami is in trouble?

MR. M. Not yet, but he will be if he's not careful. And all his friends as well. It's swimming around everywhere trying to stir up things. In the classroom, out on the streets.

ISABEL. Oh, you mean that sort of trouble. Is it really as bad as people are saying?

MR. M. There's a dangerous, reckless mood in the location. 'Specially among the young people. Very silly things are being said, Isabel, and I've got a suspicion that even sillier things are being whispered among themselves. I know Thami trusts you. I was wondering if he had told you what they were whispering about.

ISABEL. (*Shocked by what Mr. M was asking of her.*) Wow! That's a hard one you're asking for, Mr. M. Just suppose he had, do you think it would be right for me to tell you? *We* call that splitting, you know, and you're not very popular if you're caught doing it.

MR. M. It would be for his own good, Isabel.

ISABEL. Well, he hasn't ... thank God! So I don't have to deal with that one. (*Pause.*) If I ever did that to him, and he found out, that would be the end of our friendship, you know. I wish you hadn't asked me.

MR. M. (*Realizing his mistake.*) Forgive me, Isabel. I'm just over-anxious on his behalf. One silly mistake now could ruin everything. Forget that I asked you and ... please ... don't mention anything about our little chat to Thami. I'll find time to have a word with him myself.

THAMI. (*Appears. Also direct from the sports field.*) Hi, folks. Sorry I'm late.

ISABEL. I've just got here myself. Mr. M is the one who's been waiting.

THAMI. Sorry, teacher. The game went into extra time.

ISABEL. Did you win?

THAMI. No. We lost one-nil.

ISABEL. Good.

THAMI. But it was a good game. We're trying out some new combinations and they nearly worked. The chaps are really starting to come together as a team. A little more practice, that's all we need.

ISABEL. Hear that, Mr. M? What did I tell you? And look at him. Smiling! Happy! Even in defeat, a generous word for his teammates.

THAMI. What's going on?

ISABEL. Don't try to look innocent, Mbikwana. Your secret is out. Your true identity has been revealed. You are a good loser, and don't try to deny it.

THAMI. Me? You're wrong. I don't like losing.

ISABEL. It's not a question of liking or not liking, but of being able to do so without a crooked smile on your face, a knot in your stomach and murder in your heart.

THAMI. You lost your game this afternoon.

ISABEL. Whatever made you guess! We were trounced. So be careful. I'm looking for revenge.

MR. M. Good! Then let's see if you can get it in the arena of English literature. What do we deal with today?

THAMI. Nineteenth century poetry.

MR. M. (*With relish.*) Beautiful! Beautiful! Beautiful! (*Making himself comfortable.*) Whose service?

(*THAMI picks up a stone, hands behind his back, then clenched fists for Isabel to guess. SHE does. SHE wins. Their relationship is now obviously very relaxed and easy.*)

ISABEL. Gird your loins, Mbikwana. I want blood.

THAMI. I wish you the very best of luck.

ISABEL. God, I hate you.

MR. M. First service, please.

ISABEL. Right. I'll give you an easy one to start with. The Lake Poets. Name them.

THAMI. Wordsworth ...

ISABEL. Yes, he was one. Who else?

THAMI. Wordsworth and ...

ISABEL. There was only one Wordsworth.

THAMI. I pass.

ISABEL. Wordsworth, Southey and Coleridge.

THAMI. I should have guessed Coleridge!

MR. M. One–love.

ISABEL. First line of a poem by each of them please.

THAMI. Query, Mr. Umpire ... how many questions is that?

MR. M. One at a time please, Isabel.

ISABEL. Coleridge.

THAMI. "In Xanadu did Kubla Khan a stately pleasure dome decree ..."

And if you don't like that one what about:

"Tis the middle of the night by the castle clock
And the owls have awakened the crowing cock
Tu-whit Tu-whoo."

And if you're still not satisfied ...

ISABEL. Stop showing off, young man.

MR. M. One–all.

ISABEL. Wordsworth.

THAMI. "Earth has not anything to show more fair;
Dull would be he of soul who could pass by
A sight so touching in its majesty and not be moved."

MR. M. One–two.

ISABEL. Southey.

THAMI. Pass.

ISABEL. "From his brimstone bed at break of day
A-walking the devil is gone
His coat was red and his breeches were blue
And there was a hole where his tail came through"

THAMI. Hey, I like that one!

ISABEL. A poet Laureate to boot.

MR. M. Two–all.

ISABEL. One of them was expelled from school. Who was it and why?

THAMI. Wordsworth. For smoking in the lavatory.

ISABEL. (*After a good laugh.*) You're terrible, Thami. He should be penalized, Mr. Umpire ... for irreverence! It was Southey and the reason he was expelled—you're going to like this—was for writing a "precocious" essay against flogging.

THAMI. How about that!

MR. M. Three–two. Change service.

THAMI. I am not going to show you any mercy. What poet was born with deformed feet, accused of incest and died of fever while helping the Greeks fight for freedom? "A love of liberty characterizes his poems and the desire to see the fettered nations of Europe set free."

ISABEL. Byron.

THAMI. Lord Byron, if you please.

MR. M. Two–four.

ISABEL. One of your favorites.

THAMI. You bet. "Yet, freedom, Yet thy banner torn but flying,

Streams like a thunderstorm against the wind."

Do you know the Christian names of Lord Byron?

ISABEL. Oh dammit! ... it's on the tip of my tongue. Henry?

(*THAMI shakes his head.*)

ISABEL. Herbert?

THAMI. How many guesses does she get, Mr. Umpire?

ISABEL. All right, give him the point. I pass.

THAMI. George Gordon.

MR. M. Three–four.

THAMI. To whom was he unhappily married for one long year?

ISABEL. Pass.

THAMI. Anne Isabella Milbanke.

MR. M. Four–all.

THAMI. Father's occupation?

ISABEL. Pass.

THAMI. John Byron was a Captain in the Army.

MR. M. Five–four.

THAMI. What other great poet was so overcome with grief when he heard news of Lord Byron's death, that he went out and carved into a rock: "Byron is dead."

ISABEL. Matthew Arnold?

THAMI. No. Another aristocrat ... Alfred Lord Tennyson.

MR. M. Six–four. Change service.

ISABEL. Right. Whose body did your Lord Byron burn on a beach in Italy?

THAMI. Shelley.

MR. M. Four–seven.

ISABEL. And what happened to Mr. Shelley's ashes?

THAMI. In a grave beside John Keats in Rome.

MR. M. Four–eight.

ISABEL. Shelley's wife. What is she famous for?

THAMI. Which one? There were two. Harriet Westbrook, Sixteen years old, who he abandoned after three years and who drowned herself? Or number two wife—who I think is the one you're interested in—Mary Wollstonecraft, the author of *Frankenstein*.

MR. M. Four–nine.

ISABEL. How much?

MR. M. Four–nine.

ISABEL. I don't believe this! (*SHE grabs her hockey stick.*)

THAMI. (*Enjoying himself immensely.*) I crammed in two poets last night, Isabel. Guess who they were?

ISABEL. Byron and Shelley. In that case we will deal with Mr. John Keats. What profession did he abandon in order to devote himself to poetry?

THAMI. Law.

ISABEL. You're guessing and you're wrong. He qualified as a surgeon.

MR. M. Five–nine.

ISABEL. What epitaph, composed by himself, is engraved on his tombstone in Rome?

THAMI. Pass.

ISABEL. "Here lies one whose name was writ on water."

MR. M. Six–nine. Let's leave the Births, Marriages and Deaths column please. I want to hear some more poetry.

THAMI. Whose service?

MR. M. Yours.

THAMI. "I must go down to the seas again, to the lonely sea and the sky

And all I ask is a tall ship and a star to steer her by ..."

ISABEL. "And the wheel's kick and the wind's song and the white sails shaking

And a grey mist on the sea's face and a grey dawn breaking.

I must go down to the seas again, to the vagrant gypsy life

To the gull's way and the whale's way where the wind's like a whetted knife ...

THAMI. "And all I ask is a merry yarn from a laughing fellow rover

And a quiet sleep and sweet dream when the long trek's over."

MR. M. Bravo! Bravo! Bravo! But who gets the point?

ISABEL. Give it to John Masefield, Mr. Umpire. (*To Thami.*) Nineteenth century?

THAMI. He was born in 1878. To tell you the truth I couldn't resist it. You choose one.

ISABEL. "I met a traveler from an antique land
Who said: two vast and trunkless legs of stone
Stand in the desert ... near them, on the sand, half sunk, a shattered visage lies, whose frown
And wrinkled lip, and sneer of cold command
Tell that its sculptor well those passions read
Which yet survive, stamped on these lifeless things
The hand that mocked them, and the heart that fed:
And on the pedestal these words appear:

THAMI. "My name is Ozymandias, King of Kings.
Look on my works oh ye mighty, and despair!"

ISABEL. "Nothing beside remains.
'Round the decay of that colossal wreck, boundless and bare,
The lone and level sands stretch far away."

THAMI. And that point goes to Mr. Shelley.

ISABEL. (*Notebook from her schoolcase.*) You'll be interested to know, gentlemen, that Ozymandias is not a fiction of Mr. Shelley's very fertile imagination. He was a real, live Egyptian king. Rameses the Second! According to Everyman's Encyclopedia ... "One of the most famous of the Egyptian kings ... erected many monuments ... but his oppressive rule left Egypt impoverished and suffering from an incurable decline."

THAMI. What happened to the statue?

ISABEL. You mean how was it toppled?

THAMI. Yes.

ISABEL. Didn't say. Weather I suppose. And time. Two thousand four hundred B.C. ... that's over four thousand years ago. Why? What were you thinking?

THAMI. I had a book of Bible stories when I was small, and there was a picture in it showing the building of the pyramids by the slaves. Thousands of them, like ants, pulling the big blocks of stone with ropes, being guarded by soldiers with whips and spears. According to that picture the slaves must have easily outnumbered the soldiers one hundred to one. I actually tried to count them all one day but the drawing wasn't good enough for that.

ISABEL. What are you up to, Mbikwana? Trying to stir up a little social unrest in the time of the Pharoahs, are you?

THAMI. Don't joke about it, Miss Dyson. there are quite a few Ozymandiases in this country waiting to be toppled. And you'll see it happen. *We* won't leave it to time to bring them down.

MR. M. (*Has been listening to the exchange between Thami and Isabel very attentively. Trying to put a smile on it.*) Who is the *we* you speak of with such authority, Thami?

THAMI. The People.

MR. M. (*Recognition.*) Yes, yes, yes, of course ... I should have known. "The People" ... with a capital P. Does that include me? Am I one of "The People?"

THAMI. If you choose to be.

MR. M. I've got to choose, have I? My black skin doesn't confer automatic membership. So how do I go about choosing?

THAMI. By identifying with the fight for our freedom.

MR. M. As simple as that? Then I am most definitely one of "The People." I want our freedom as much as any of you. In fact, I was fighting for it in my own small way long before you were born! But I've got a small problem. Does that noble fight of ours really have to stoop to pulling down a few silly statues? Where do you get the idea that we, The People, want you to do that for us?

THAMI. (*Trying.*) They are not our heroes, teacher.

MR. M. They are not our statues, Thami! Wouldn't it be better for us to rather put our energies into erecting a few of our own? We've also got heroes, you know.

THAMI. Like who, Mr. M? Nelson Mandela? (*Shaking his head with disbelief.*) Hey! *They* would pull *that* statue down so fast ...

MR. M. (*Cutting him.*) In which case they would be just as guilty of gross vandalism ... because that it what it will be, regardless of who does it to whom. Destroying somebody else's property is inexcusable behavior! No, Thami. As one of the People you claim to be acting for, I raise my hand in protest. Please don't pull down any statues on my behalf. Don't use me as an excuse for an act of lawlessness. If you want to do something "revolutionary" for me let us sit down and discuss it, because I have a few constructive alternatives I would like to suggest. Do I make myself clear?

THAMI. Yes, teacher.

MR. M. Good. I'm glad we understand each other.

ISABEL. (*Intervening.*) So, what's next? Mr. M? How about singling out a few specific authors who we know will definitely come up. Like Dickens. I bet you anything you like there'll be questions about him and his work.

MR. M. Good idea. We'll concentrate on novelists. A short list of hot favorites.

ISABEL. Thomas Hardy ... Jane Austen ... who else, Thami?

MR. M. Put your heads together and make a list. I want twenty names. Divide it between the two of you and get to work. I must be on my way.

ISABEL. Just before you go, Mr. M, I've got an invitation for you and Thami from my mom and dad. Would the two of you like to come to tea one afternoon?

MR. M. What a lovely idea!

ISABEL. They've had enough of me going on and on about the all-knowing Mr. M and his brilliant protege Thami. They want to meet you for themselves. Thami? All right with you?

MR. M. Of course we accept, Isabel. It will be a pleasure and a privilege for us to meet Mr. and Mrs. Dyson. Tell them we accept most gratefully.

ISABEL. Next Sunday.

MR. M. Perfect.

ISABEL. Thami?

MR. M. Don't worry about him, Isabel. I'll put it in my diary and remind him at school. (*Leaves.*)

ISABEL. (*Sensitive to a change in mood in Thami.*) I think you'll like my folks. My mom's a bit on the reserved side but that's just because she's basically very shy. But you and my dad should get on well. Start talking sport with him and he won't let you go. He played cricket for E.P., you know. (*Pause.*) You will come, won't you?

THAMI. (*Edged to his voice.*) Did you hear Mr. M? " A delight and a privilege! We accept most gratefully." (*Writing in his notebook.*) Charles Dickens ... Thomas Hardy ... Jane Austen ...

ISABEL. Was he speaking for you as well?

THAMI. He speaks for me on nothing!

ISABEL. Relax ... I know that. That's why I tried to ask you separately and why I'll ask you again. Would you like to come to tea next Sunday to meet my family? It's not a polite invitation. They really want to meet you.

THAMI. Me? Why? Are they starting to get nervous?

ISABEL. Oh come off it, Thami. Don't be like that. They're always nervous when it comes to me. But this time it happens to be genuine interest. I've told you. I talk about you at home. They know I have a good time with you ... that we're a team ... which they are now very proud of, incidentally ... and that we're cramming like lunatics so

that we can put up a good show at the festival. Is it so
strange that they want to meet you after all that? Honestly,
sometimes dealing with the two of you is like walking on
a tight rope. I'm always scared I'm going to put a foot
wrong and ... well, I just *hate* being scared like that. (*A
few seconds of truculent silence between the two of them.*)
What's going on, Thami? Between you two? There's
something very wrong, isn't there?

THAMI. No more than usual.

ISABEL. No, you don't! A hell of a lot more than
usual and don't deny it because it's getting to be pretty
obvious. I mean I know he gets on your nerves. I knew
that the first day we met. But it's more than that now.
These past couple of meetings I've caught you looking at
him, watching him in a ... I don't know ... in a sort of
hard way. Very critical. Not just once. Many times. Do
you know you're doing it?

(*Shrug of shoulders from THAMI.*)

ISABEL. Well, if you know it or not you are. And now
he's started as well.

THAMI. What do you mean?

ISABEL. He's watching you.

THAMI. So? He can watch me as much as he likes.
I've got nothing to hide. Even if I had he'd be the last
person to find out. He sees nothing, Isabel.

ISABEL. I think you are very wrong.

THAMI. No, I'm not. That's his trouble. He's got eyes
and ears but he sees nothing and hears nothing.

ISABEL. Go on. Please. (*Pause.*) I mean it, Thami. I
want to know what's going on.

THAMI. He is out of touch with what is really
happening to us blacks and the way we feel about things.
He thinks the world is still the way it was when he was

young. It's not! It's different now, but he's too blind to see it. He doesn't open his eyes and ears and see what is happening around him or listen to what people are saying.

ISABEL. What are they saying?

THAMI. They've got no patience left, Isabel. They want change. They want it now!

ISABEL. But he agrees with that. He never stops saying it himself.

THAMI. No. His ideas about change are the old fashioned ones. And what have they achieved? Nothing. We are worse off now than we ever were. The people don't want to listen to his kind of talk anymore.

ISABEL. I'm still lost, Thami. What kind of talk is that?

THAMI. You've just heard it, Isabel. It calls our struggle vandalism and lawless behavior. It's the sort of talk that expects us to do nothing and wait quietly for White South Africa to wake up. If we listen to it our grandchildren still won't know what it means to be free.

ISABEL. And those old-fashioned ideas of his ... are we one of them?

THAMI. What do you mean?

ISABEL. You and me. The competition.

THAMI. Let's change the subject, Isabel. (*His notebook.*) Charles Dickens ... Thomas Hardy ... Jane Austen ...

ISABEL. No! You can't do that! I'm involved. I've got a right to know. Are we an old fashioned idea?

THAMI. Not our friendship. That is our decision, our choice.

ISABEL. And the competition.

THAMI. (*Uncertain of himself.*) Maybe ... I'm not sure. I need time to think about it.

ISABEL. (*Foreboding.*) Oh boy. This doesn't sound so good. You've got to talk to him, Thami.

THAMI. He won't listen.

ISABEL. Make him listen!

THAMI. It doesn't work that way with us, Isabel. You can't just stand up and tell your teacher he's got the wrong ideas.

ISABEL. Well, that's just your bad luck because you are going to have to do it. Even if it means breaking sacred rules and traditions, you have got to stand up and have it out with him. I don't think you realize what all of this means to him. It's a hell of a lot more than just an "old-fashioned idea" as far as he's concerned. This competition, you and me, but especially you, Thami Mbikwana, has become a sort of crowning achievement to his life as a teacher. It's become a sort of symbol for him, and if it were to all suddenly collapse ...! No. I don't want to think about it.

THAMI. (*Flash of anger and impatience.*) Then don't! Please leave it alone now and just let's get on with whatever it is we've got to do .

ISABEL. Right, if that's the way you want it ... (*Her notebook.*) ... Charles Dickens, Thomas Hardy, Jane Austen ... who else?

THAMI. I'm sorry. I know you're only trying to help but you've got to understand that it's not just a personal issue between him and me. That would be easy. I don't think I would care then. Just wait for the end of the year and then get out of that classroom and that school as fast as I can. But there is more to it than that. I've told you before: sitting in a classroom doesn't mean the same thing to me that it does to you. That classroom is a political reality in my life ... it's a part of the whole political system we're up against and Mr. M has chosen to identify with it.

ISABEL. (*Trying a new tack.*) All right. I believe you. I accept everything you said ... about him, your relationship, the situation. No arguments. Okay? But doesn't all of that only make it still more important that the two of you start talking to each other? I know *he* wants to, but he doesn't know how to start. It's *so* sad ... because I can see him trying to reach out to you. Show him how it's done. Make the first move. Oh Thami, don't let it go wrong between the two of you. That's just about the worst thing I could imagine. We all need each other.

THAMI. I don't need him.

ISABEL. I think you do, just as much as he ...

THAMI. Don't tell me what I need, Isabel! And stop telling me what to do! You don't know what my life is about, so keep your advice to yourself.

ISABEL. I'm sorry. I don't mean to interfere. I thought we were a team and that what involved you two concerned me as well. I'll mind my own business in future. (*SHE is deeply hurt. SHE collects her things.*) Let's leave it at that then. See you next week ... I hope! (*Starts to leave, stops, returns and confronts him.*) You used the word friendship a few minutes ago. It's a beautiful word and I'll do anything to make it true for us. But don't let's cheat, Thami. If we can't be open and honest with each other and say what is in our hearts, we've got no right to use it. (*SHE leaves.*)

Scene 6

THAMI. (*Alone. Singing.*)
MASIYE MASIYE SKOLWENI
MASIYE MASIYE SKOLWENI
ESKOLWENI SASAKHAYA
ESKOLWENI SASAKHAYA (*Repeat.*)

GONGO GONGO

IYAKHALA INTSIMBI
GONGO GONGO
IYAKHALA INTSIMBI

(*Translating.*)

COME, COME, LET'S GO TO SCHOOL
LET'S GO TO OUR VERY OWN SCHOOL
GONGO GONGO
THE BELL IS RINGING
GONGO GONGO
THE BELL IS CALLING!

Singing that at the top of his voice and holding his slate under his arm, seven-year-old Thami Mbikwana marched proudly with the other children every morning into his classroom.

Gongo Gongo The school bell is ringing!

And what a wonderful sound that was for me. Starting with the little farm school, I remember my school bells like beautiful voices calling to me all through my childhood ... and I came running when they did. You should have seen me, man. In junior school I was the first one at the gates every morning. I was waiting there when the caretaker came to unlock them. Oh yes! Young Thami was a very eager scholar. And what made it even better, he was also one of the clever ones. "A most particularly promising pupil" is how one of my school reports described me. My first real scholastic achievement was a composition I wrote about myself in Standard Two. Not only did it get me top marks in the class, the teacher was so proud of me, she made me read it out to the whole school at assembly.

(*His composition.*) "The story of my life so far. By Thami Mbikwana. The story of my life so far is not yet finished because I am only ten years old and I am going to live a long long time.

"I come from King Williamstown. My father is Amos Mbikwana and he works very hard for the baas on the railway. I am also going to work very hard and get good marks in all my classes and make my teacher very happy. The story of my life so far has also got a very happy ending because when I am big I am going to be a doctor so that I can help people. I will drive to the hospital every day in a big, white ambulance full of nurses. I will make black people better free of charge. The white people must pay me for my medicine because they have got lots of money. That way I will also get lots of money. My mother and my father will stop working and come and live with me in a big house. That is the story of my life up to where I am in Standard Two."

I must bring my story up to date because there have been some changes and developments since little Thami wrote those hopeful words eight years ago. To start with, I don't think I want to be a doctor anymore. That praiseworthy ambition has unfortunately died in me. It still upsets me very much when I think about the pain and suffering of my people, but I realize now that what causes most of it is not an illness that can be cured by the pills and bottles of medicine they hand out at the clinic. I don't need to go to university to learn what my people really need is a strong double-dose of that traditional old Xhosa remedy called Inkululeko. Freedom. So right now I'm not sure what I want to be any more. It's hard, you see, for us "bright young blacks" to dream about wonderful careers as doctors, or lawyers when we keep waking up in a world which doesn't allow the majority of our people any dreams at all. But to get back to my composition, I did try my best to keep that promise I made in it. For a long time ... Standard Three, Standard Four, Standard Five ... I did work very hard and I did get good marks in all my subjects. This "most particularly promising pupil" made a lot of teachers very happy.

I'm sorry to say but I can't do it anymore. I have tried very hard, believe me, but it is not as simple and easy as it used to be to sit behind that desk and listen to the teacher. That little world of the classroom where I used to be happy, where they used to pat me on the head and say: Little Thami, You'll go far! ...That little room of wonderful promises, where I used to feel so safe, has become a place I don't trust anymore. Now I sit at my desk like an animal that has smelt danger, heard something moving in the bushes and knows it must be very, very careful.

At the beginning of this year the Inspector of Bantu Schools in the Cape Midlands Region, Mr. Dawid Grobbelaar—he makes us call him Oom Dawie—came to give us Standard Tens his usual pep talk. He does it every year. We know Oom Dawie well. He's been coming to Zolile for a long time. When he walked into our classroom we all jumped up as usual but he didn't want any of that. "Sit, sit. I'm not a bloody sergeant major." Oom Dawie believes he knows how to talk to us. He loosened his tie, took off his jacket and rolled up his sleeves. It was a very hot day.

"Dis better. Nou kan ons lekker gesels. Boys and girls or maybe I should say 'young men' and 'young women' now, because you are coming to the end of your time behind those desks ... you are special! You are the elite! We have educated you because we want you to be major shareholders in the future of this wonderful Republic of ours. In fact, we want *all* the peoples of South Africa to share in that future ... black, white, brown, yellow and if there are some green ones out there, then them as well." Ho! Ho! Ho!

I don't remember much about what he said after that because my head was trying to deal with that one word: the Future! He kept using it ... "our future," "the country's future," "A wonderful future of peace and prosperity." What does he really mean, I kept asking myself? Why does my heart go hard and tight as a stone when he says it? I look around me in the location at the men and women who went out into that "wonderful future" before me. What do I see? Happy and contented shareholders in this exciting enterprise called the Republic of South Africa? No. I see a generation of tired, defeated men and women crawling back to their miserable little pondocks at the end of a day's work for the white baas or madam. And those are the lucky ones. They've at least got work. Most of them are just sitting around wasting away their lives while they wait helplessly for a miracle to feed their families, a miracle that never comes.

Those men and women are our fathers and mothers. We have grown up watching their humiliation. We have to live everyday with the sight of them begging for food in this land of their birth, and their parents' birth ... all the way back to the first proud ancestors of our people. Black people lived on this land for centuries before any white settler had landed! Does Oom Dawie think we are blind? That when we walk through the streets of the white town we do not see the big houses and the beautiful gardens with their swimming pools full of laughing people, and compare it with what we've got, what we have to call home? Or does Oom Dawie just think we are very stupid? That in spite of the wonderful education he has given us, we can't use the simple arithmetic of add and subtract, multiply and divide to work out the rightful share of twenty five million black people?

Do you understand me, good people? Do you understand now why it is not as easy as it used to be to sit behind that

desk and learn only what Oom Dawie has decided I must
know? My head is rebellious. It refuses now to remember
when the Dutch landed, and the Huguenots landed, and the
British landed. It has already forgotten when the Old Union
became the proud young Republic. But it does know what
happened in Kliptown in 1955, in Sharpville on 21st
March, 1960 and in Soweto on the 16th of June, 1976. Do
you? Better find out, because those are dates your children
will have to learn one day. We don't need Zolile
classrooms anymore. We know now what they really are ...
traps which have been carefully set to catch our minds, our
souls. No, good people. We have woken up at last. We
have found another school ... the streets, the little rooms,
the funeral parlors of the location ... anywhere the people
meet and whisper names we have been told to forget, the
dates of event they try to tell us never happened, and the
speeches they try to say were never made.

Those are the lessons we are eager and proud to learn,
because they are lessons about *our* history, about *our*
heroes. But the time for whispering them is past.
Tomorrow we start shouting.

AMANDLA!

ACT II

Scene 1

ISABEL and THAMI. SHE has books and papers. Behind a relaxed and easy manner, SHE watches Thami carefully.

ISABEL. What I've done is write out a sort of condensed biography of all of them ... you know, the usual stuff ... date of birth, where they were born, where they died, who they married ... et cetera et cetera. My dad made copies for you and Mr. M. Sit. (*Hands over a set of papers to Thami.*) You okay?

THAMI. Ja, ja.

ISABEL. For example ... (*Reading.*) ... Bronte sisters ... I lumped them all together ... Charlotte 1816-1855; Emily 1818-1848; Anne 1820-1849 ... Can you believe that: Not one of them reached the age of forty. Anne died when she was twenty-nine, Emily when she was thirty, and Charlotte reached the ripe old age of thirty-nine! Family home: Haworth, Yorkshire. First publication a joint volume of verse ... "Poems by Currer, Ellis and Acton Bell." All novels published under these nommes de plume. Charlotte the most prolific ... (*Abandoning the notes.*) Why am I doing this? You're not listening to me.

THAMI. Sorry.

ISABEL. (*SHE waits for more, but that is all she gets.*) So? Should I carry on wasting my breath or do you want to say something?

THAMI. No, I must talk.

ISABEL. Good. I'm ready to listen.

THAMI. I don't know where to begin.

ISABEL. The deep end. Take my advice, go to the deep end and just jump right in. That's how I learnt to swim.

THAMI. No. I want to speak carefully because I don't want you to get the wrong ideas about what's happening and what I'm going to say. It's not like it's your fault, that it's because of anything you said or did ... you know what I mean?

ISABEL. You don't want me to take personally whatever it is you are finding so hard to tell me.

THAMI. That's right. It's not about you and me personally. I've had a good time with you, Isabel.

ISABEL. And I've had an important one with you.

THAMI. If it was just you and me, there wouldn't be a problem.

ISABEL. We've got a problem have we?

THAMI. I have.

ISABEL. (*Losing patience.*) Oh for God's sake, Thami. Stop trying to spare my feelings and just say it. If you are trying to tell me that I've been wasting my breath for a lot longer than just this afternoon ... just go ahead and say it! I'm not a child. I can take it. Because that is what you are trying to tell me, isn't it? That it's all off.

THAMI. Yes.

ISABEL. The great literary quiz team is no more. You are pulling out of the competition.

THAMI. Yes.

ISABEL. You shouldn't have made it so hard for yourself, Thami. It doesn't come as all that big a surprise. I've had a feeling that something was going to go wrong somewhere. Been a strange time these past few weeks, hasn't it? At home, at school, in the shop ... everywhere! Things I've been seeing and doing my whole life, just don't feel right anymore. Like my Saturday chats with Samuel—I told you about him, remember, he delivers for my dad—well you should have heard the last one. It was excruciating. It felt so false, and forced, and when I listened to what I was saying and how I was saying it ... oh my God! Sounded as if I thought I was talking to a ten year old. Halfway through our misery my dad barged in and told me not to waste Samuel's time because he had work to do, which, of course, led to a flaming row between me and my dad ... Am I changing, Thami? My dad says I am.   ←

THAMI. In what way?

ISABEL. Forget it. The only thing I *do* know at this moment is that I don't very much like the way anything feels right now, starting with myself. So have you told Mr. M yet?

THAMI. No.

ISABEL. Good luck. I don't envy you that little conversation. If I'm finding the news a bit hard to digest, I don't know what he is going to do with it. I've just got to accept it. I doubt very much if he will.

THAMI. He's got no choice, Isabel. I've decided and that's the end of it.

ISABEL. So do you think we can at least talk about it? Help me to understand? Because to be absolutely honest with you, Thami, I don't think I do. You're not the only one with a problem. What Mr. M had to say about the team and the whole idea made a hell of a lot of sense to me. You owe it to me, Thami. A lot more than just my spare time is involved.

THAMI. Talk about what? Don't you know what is going on?

ISABEL. Don't be stupid, Thami! Of course I do! You'd have to be pretty dumb not to know that the dreaded "unrest" has finally reached us as well.

THAMI. We don't call it that. Our word for it is "Isiqalo" ... The Beginning.

ISABEL. All right then, "the Beginning." I don't care what it's called. All I'm asking you to do is explain to me how the two of us learning some poetry, cramming in potted bios ... interferes with all of that.

THAMI. Please just calm down and listen to me! I know you're angry and I don't blame you. I would be as well. But you must understand that pulling out of this competition is just a small side issue. There was a meeting in the location last night. It was decided to call for a general stay-at-home. We start boycotting classes tomorrow as part of that campaign.

ISABEL. Does Mr. M know about all of this?

THAMI. I think he does now.

ISABEL. Wasn't he at that meeting?

THAMI. The meeting was organized by the Comrades. He wasn't welcome.

ISABEL. Because his ideas are old-fashioned.

THAMI. Yes.

ISABEL. School boycott! Comrades! So our safe, contented little Camdeboo is really going to find out what it's all about. How long do you think it will last?

THAMI. I don't know. It's hard to say.

ISABEL. A week.

THAMI. No. It will be longer.

ISABEL. A month? Two months?

THAMI. We'll go back to school when the authorities scrap Bantu Education and recognize and negotiate with Student Committees. That was the resolution last night.

ISABEL. But when the boycott and ... you know ...everything is all over, could we carry on then, if there was still time?

THAMI. I hadn't thought about that.

ISABEL. So think about it. Please.

THAMI. (*Nervous about a commitment.*) It's hard to say, Isabel ... but ja maybe we could ... I'm not sure.

ISABEL. Not much enthusiasm there, Mr. Mbikwana! You're right. Why worry about a stupid competition? It will most probably be too late anyway. So that's it then. Let's just say we gave ourselves a crash course in English literature. Could have done a lot worse with our spare time, couldn't we? I enjoyed myself. I read a lot of beautiful poetry I might never have got around to. (*Uncertain of herself.*) It doesn't mean the end of everything though, does it? I mean, we can go on meeting, just as friends?

THAMI. (*Warily.*) When?

ISABEL. Oh ... I mean, you know, like any time. Next week! (*Pause.*) I'm not talking about the competition, Thami. I accept that it's dead. I think it's a pity ... but so what? I'm talking now about you and me just as friends. (*SHE waits. SHE realizes. SHE collects herself.*) So our friendship *is* an old-fashioned idea after all. Well don't waste your time here. You better get going and look after ... whatever it is that's beginning. And good luck!

(*THAMI starts to go.*)

ISABEL. No! Thami come back here!! (*Struggling ineffectually to control her anger and pain.*) There is something very stupid somewhere and it's most probably me but I can't help it ... *It just doesn't make sense!* I know it does to you and I'm sure it's just my white selfishness and ignorance that is stopping me from understanding *but it still doesn't make sense.* Why can't we go on seeing each other and meeting as friends? Tell me what is wrong with our friendship?

THAMI. You're putting words in my mouth, Isabel. I didn't say there was anything wrong with it. But others will not see it the way we do.

ISABEL. Who? Your Comrades?

THAMI. Yes.

ISABEL. And they are going to decide whether we can or can't be friends!

THAMI. I was right. You don't understand what's going on.

ISABEL. And you're certainly not helping me to.

THAMI. (*Trying.*) ... Visiting you like this is dangerous. People talk. Your maid, Usispumla ... has seen me. She could mention, just innocently but to the wrong person, that Thami Mbikwana is visiting and having tea with the white people she works for.

ISABEL. And of course that is such a big crime!

THAMI. In the eyes of the location ... Yes! My world is also changing, Isabel. I'm breaking the boycott by being here. The Comrades don't want any mixing with the whites. They have ordered that contact must be kept at a minimum.

ISABEL. And you go along with that.

THAMI. Yes.

ISABEL. Happily!

THAMI. (*Goaded by her lack of understanding.*) Yes! I go along happily with that!!

ISABEL. Hell, Thami, this great Beginning of yours sounds like ... (*Shakes her head.*) ... I don't know. Other people deciding who can and who can't be your friends, what you must do and what you can't do. Is this the freedom you've been talking to me about? That you were going to fight for?

MR. M. (*Enters quietly. His stillness is a disturbing contrast to the bustle and energy we have come to associate with him.*) Don't let me interrupt you. Please carry on. (*To Thami.*) I'm most interested in your reply to that question. (*Pause.*) I think he's forgotten what it was, Isabel. Ask him again.

ISABEL. (*Backing out of the confrontation.*) No. Forget it.

MR. M. (*Persisting.*) Isabel was asking you how you managed to reconcile your desire for freedom with what the Comrades are doing.

ISABEL. I said forget it, Mr. M. I'm not interested anymore.

MR. M. (*Insistent.*) But I am.

THAMI. The Comrades are imposing a discipline which our struggle needs at this point. There is no comparison between that and the total denial of our freedom by the white government. They have been forcing on us an inferior education in order to keep us permanently suppressed. When our struggle is successful there will be no more need for the discipline the Comrades are demanding.

MR. M. (*Grudging admiration.*) Oh, Thami ... you learn your lessons so well! The "revolution" has only just begun and you are already word perfect. So then tell me, do you think I agree with this inferior "Bantu Education" that is being forced on you?

THAMI. You teach it.

MR. M. But unhappily so! Most unhappily, unhappily so! Don't you know that? Did you have your fingers in your ears the thousand times I've said so in the classroom? Where were you when I stood there and said I regarded it as my duty, my deepest obligation to you young men and women to sabotage it, and that my conscience would not let me rest until I had succeeded. And I have! Yes, I have succeeded! I have got irrefutable proof of my success. You! Yes. You can stand here and accuse me, unjustly, because I have also had a struggle and I have won mine. I have liberated your mind in spite of what the Bantu education was trying to do to it. Your mouthful of big words and long sentences which the not-so-clever Comrades are asking you to speak and write for them, your wonderful eloquence at last night's meeting which got them all so excited—yes, I heard about it!—you must thank me for all of that, Thami.

THAMI. No, I don't. You never taught me those lessons.

MR. M. Oh, I see. You have got other teachers have you?

THAMI. Yes. Yours were lessons in whispering. There are men now who are teaching us to shout. Those little tricks and jokes of yours in the classroom liberated nothing. The struggle doesn't need the big English words you taught me how to spell.

MR. M. Be careful, Thami. Be careful! Be careful! Don't scorn words. They are sacred! Magical! Yes, they are. Do you know that without words a man can't think? Yes, It's true. Take that thought back with you as a present from the despised Mr. M and share it with the Comrades. Tell them the difference between a man and an animal is that man thinks, and he thinks with words. Consider the mighty ox. Four powerful legs, massive shoulders, and a beautiful thick hide that gave our warriors shields to protect them when they went into battle. Think of his beautiful head, Thami, the long horns, the terrible bellow from his lungs when he charges a rival! *But it has got no words and therefore it is stupid!* And along comes that funny little, hairless animal that has got only two thin legs, no horns and a skin worth nothing and he tells that ox what to do. He is its master and he is that because he can speak! If the struggle needs weapons give it words, Thami. Stones and petrol bombs can't get inside those armored cars. Words can. They can do something even more devastating than that ... they can get inside the heads of those inside the armored cars. I speak to you like this because if I have faith in anything, it is faith in the power of the word. Like my master, the great Confucius, I believe that, using only words, a man can right a wrong and judge and execute the wrongdoer. You are meant to use words like that. Talk to others. Bring them back into the classroom. They will listen to you. They look up to you as a leader.

THAMI. No I won't. You talk about them as if they were a lot of sheep waiting to be led. They know what they are doing. They'd call me a traitor if I tried to persuade them otherwise.

MR. M. Then listen carefully, Thami. I have received instructions from the department to make a list of all those who take part in the boycott. Do you know what they will do with that list when all this is over? ... because don't fool yourself, Thami, it will be. When your boycott comes to an inglorious end like all the others ... they will make all of you apply for re-admission and if your name is on that list ... (*HE leave the rest unspoken.*)

THAMI. Will you do it? Will you make that list for them?

MR. M. That is none of your business.

THAMI. Then don't ask me questions about mine.

MR. M. (*His control finally snaps. HE explodes with anger and bitterness.*) Yes, I will! I will ask you all the questions I like. And you know why? Because I am a man and you are a boy. And if you are not in that classroom tomorrow you will be a very, very silly boy.

THAMI. Then don't call me names, Mr. M.

MR. M. No? Then what must I call you? Comrade Thami? Never! You are a silly boy now, and without an education you will grow up to be a stupid man!

(*For a moment it looks as if THAMI is going to leave without saying anything more, but HE changes his mind and confronts Mr. M for the last time.*)

THAMI. The others called *you* names at the meeting last night. Did your spies tell you that? Government stooge, sell-out, collaborator. They said you licked the white man's arse and would even eat his shit if it meant keeping your job. Did your spies tell you that I tried to stop them saying those things? Don't wait until tomorrow to make your list, Mr. M. You can start now. Write down the first name: Thami Mbikwana. (*HE leaves.*)

(*A few seconds of silence after Thami's departure. ISABEL makes a move towards Mr. M but HE raises his hand sharply, stopping her, keeping her at a distance.*)

ISABEL. This fucking country! (*SHE leaves.*)

Scene 2

MR M alone. To start with, the mood is one of quiet, vacant disbelief.

MR. M. It was like being in a nightmare. I was trying to get to the school, I knew that if I didn't hurry I was going to be late so I *had to get to the school* ... but every road I took was blocked by policemen and soldiers with their guns ready, or comrades building barricades. First I tried Jubulani Street, then I turned into Kwaza Rd. and then Lamini St. ... and then I gave up and just wandered around aimlessly, helplessly, watching my world go mad and set itself on fire. Everywhere I went ... overturned buses, looted bread vans, the government offices ... everything burning and the children dancing around rattling boxes of matches and shouting Tshisa Qhumisa! Tshisa Qhumisa! Qhumisa! ... and then running for their lives when the police armored cars appeared. They were everywhere, crawling around in the smoke like giant dung-beetles looking for shit to eat.

I ended up on the corner where Mrs. Makatini always sits selling vetkoek and prickly pears to people waiting for the bus. The only person there was little Sipho Fondini from Standard Six, writing on the wall: "Liberation First, then Education." He saw me and he called out: "Is the spelling right, Mr. M?" And he meant it! The young eyes in that smoke-stained little face were terribly serious.

Somewhere else a police van raced past me crowded with children who should have also been in their desks in school. Their hands waved desperately through the bar, their voices called out: "Teacher! Teacher! Help us! Tell our mothers. Tell our fathers." 'No Anela," I said. "This is too much now. Just stand here and close your eyes and wait until you wake up and find your world the way it was." But that didn't happen. A police car came around the corner and suddenly there were children everywhere throwing stones, and tear gas bombs falling all around and I knew that I wasn't dreaming, that I was coughing and choking and hanging on to a lamp-post in the real world. No! no!

Do something, Anela. Do something. Stop the madness! Stop the madness.

Scene 3

MR. M alone in Number One Classroom. HE is ringing his school bell wildly.

MR. M. Come to school! Come to school! Before they kill you all, come to school! (*Silence. MR. M looks around the empty classroom. HE goes to his table, and after composing himself, opens the class register and reads*

*out the names as he did every morning at the start of a new
school day.*)

Johnny Awu, living or dead? Christopher Bandla, living
or dead? Zandile Cwati, living or dead? Semphiwe
Dambuza ... Ronald Gxasheka ... Noloyiso Mfundeweni ...
Steven Gaika ...Zachariah Jabavu ... Thami ... Thami
Mbikwana ... (*Pause.*) Living or dead?

How many young souls do I have present this morning?
There are a lot of well-aimed stray bullets flying around on
the streets out there. Is that why this silence is so ...
heavy?

But what can I teach you? (*Picks up his little black
dictionary on the table.*) My lessons were meant to help
you in *this* world. I wanted you to know how to read and
write and talk in *this* world of living, stupid, cruel men.
(*Helpless gesture.*) Now? Oh my children! I have no
lessons that will be of any use to you now. Mr. M and all
of his wonderful words are ... useless, useless, useless!

(*The SOUND of breaking glass. Stones land in the
classroom. MR. M picks up one.*) No! One of you is still
alive. Ghosts don't throw stones with hot, sweating young
hands. (*Grabs the bell and rings it wildly again.*) Come to
school! Come to school!

THAMI. (*Appears. Quietly.*) Stop ringing that bell,
Mr. M.

MR. M. Why? It's only the school bell, Thami. I
thought you liked the sound of it. You once told me it was
almost as good as music ... don't you remember?

THAMI. You are provoking the Comrades with it.

MR. M. No, Thami. I am summoning the Comrades
with it.

THAMI. They say you are ringing the bell to taunt
them. You are openly defying the boycott by being here in
the school.

MR. M. I ring this bell because according to my watch it is school time and I am a teacher and those desks are empty! I will go on ringing it as I have been doing these past two weeks, at the end of every lesson. And you can tell the Comrades that I will be back here ringing it tomorrow and the day after tomorrow and for as many days after that as it takes for this world to come to its senses. Is that the only reason you've come? To tell me to stop ringing the school bell?

THAMI. No.

MR. M. You haven't come for a lesson, have you?

THAMI. No, I haven't.

MR. M. Of course not. What's the matter with me. Slogans don't need much in the way of grammar, do they? As for these ... (*The stone in his hand.*) No, you don't need me for lessons in stone throwing either. You've already got teachers in those very revolutionary subjects haven't you. (*Picks up his dictionary ... the stone in one hand, the book in the other.*) You know something interesting, Thami ... if you put these two on a scale I think you would find that they weighed just about the same. But in this hand I am holding the whole English language. This ... (*The stone.*) ... is just *one* word in that language. It's true! All that wonderful poetry that you and Isabel tried to cram into your beautiful heads ... in here! Twenty-six letters, sixty thousand words. The greatest souls the world has ever known were able to open the floodgates of their ecstasy, their despair, their joy! ... with words in this little book. Aren't you tempted? I was. (*Opens the book at the fly-leaf and reads.*) "Anela Myalatya. Cookhouse. 1947" One of the first books I ever bought. (*Impulsively.*) I want you to have it.

THAMI. (*Ignoring the offered book.*) I've come here to warn you.

MR. M. You've already done that and I've already told you that you are wasting your breath. Now take your stones and go. There are a lot of unbroken windows left.

THAMI. I'm not talking about the bell now. It's more serious than that.

MR. M. In my life nothing is more serious than ringing the school bell.

THAMI. There was a meeting last night. Somebody stood up and denounced you as an informer.

(*Pause. THAMI waits. MR. M says nothing.*)

THAMI. He said you gave names to the police.

(*MR. M says nothing.*)

THAMI. Everybody is talking about it this morning. You are in big danger.

MR. M. Why are you telling me all this?

THAMI. So that you can save yourself. There is a plan to march to the school and burn it down. If they find you here ... (*Pause.*)

MR. M. Go on. (*Violently.*) If they find me here *what?*

THAMI. They will kill you.

MR. M. (*He writes on the blackboard.*) "They will kill me." That's better. Remember what I taught you ... if you've got a problem, put it into words so that you can look at it, handle it, and ultimately solve it. They will kill me! You are right. That is very serious. So then ... what must I do? Must I run away and hide somewhere?

THAMI. No, they will find you. You must join the boycott.

MR. M. (*He writes on the blackboard.*) "Solution: Join the Boycott." I'm listening.

THAMI. Let me go back and tell them that we have had a long talk and that you have realized you were wrong and have decided to join us. Let me say that you will sign the declaration and that you won't have anything to do with the school until all demands have been met.

MR. M. And they will agree to that? Accept me as one of them even though it is believed that I am an informer?

THAMI. I will tell them you are innocent. That I confronted you with the charge and that you denied it and that I believe you.

MR. M. I see. (*Studying Thami intently.*) *You* don't believe that I am an informer.

THAMI. No.

MR. M. Won't you be taking a chance in defending me like that? Mightn't they end up suspecting you?

THAMI. They'll believe me. I'll make them believe me.

MR. M. You can't be sure. Mobs don't listen to reason, Thami. Hasn't your revolution already taught you that? Why take a chance like that to save a collaborator? Why do you want to do all this for me?

THAMI. (*Avoiding Mr. M's eyes.*) I'm not doing it for you. I'm doing it for the Struggle. Our Cause will suffer if we falsely accuse and hurt innocent people.

MR. M. I see. My "execution" would be an embarrassment to the Cause. I apologize, Thami. For a moment I allowed myself to thing that you were doing it because we were ... who we are ... the "all-knowing Mr. M and his brilliant protege Thami!" I was so proud of us when Isabel called us that.

Well, young Comrade, you have got nothing to worry about. Let them come and do whatever it is they want to. Your Cause won't be embarrassed because, you see, they won't be "hurting" an innocent man.

(*HE makes his confession simply and truthfully.*)
That's right, Thami. I am guilty. I did go to the police. I
sat down in Captain Lategan's office and told him I felt it
was my duty to report the presence in our community of
strangers from the north. I told him that I had reason to
believe that they were behind the present unrest. I gave the
Captain names and addresses. He thanked me and offered me
money for the information, which I refused.

(*Pause.*) Why do you look at me like that? Isn't that
what you expected from me? ... A government stooge, a
sell-out, an arse-licker? Isn't that what you were all secretly
hoping I would do ... so that you could be proved right?
(*Appalled.*) Is that why I did it? Out of spite? Can a man
destroy himself, his life for a reason as petty as that?

I sat here before going to the police station saying to
myself that it was my duty, to my conscience, to you, to
the whole community to do whatever I could to put an end
to this madness of boycotts and arson, mob violence and
lawlessness ... and maybe that is true ... but only maybe
... because, Thami, the truth is that I was so lonely! You
had deserted me. I was so jealous of those who had taken
you away. *Now*, I've *really* lost you, haven't I? Yes. I can
see it in your eyes. You'll never forgive me for doing that,
will you?

You know, Thami, I'd sell my soul to have you all
back behind your desks for one last lesson. Yes. If the devil
thought it was worth having and offered me that in
exchange ... one lesson! He could have my soul. So then
it's all over! Because this ... (*The classroom.*) ... is all
there was for me. This was my home, my life, my one and
only ambition ... to be a good teacher! (*His dictionary.*)
Anela Myalata, twenty years old, from Cookhouse, wanted
to be that the way your friends wanted to be big soccer
stars playing for Kaizer Chiefs! That ambition goes back to

when he was just a skinny little ten-year-old pissing on a small grey bush at the top of the Wapadsberg Pass.

We were on our way to a rugby match at Somerset East. The lorry stopped at the top of the mountain so that we could stretch our legs and relieve ourselves. It was a hard ride on the back of that lorry. The road hadn't been tarred yet. So there I was, ten years old and sighing with relief as I aimed for the little bush. It was a hot day. The sun right over our heads ... not a cloud in the vast blue sky. I looked out ... it's very high up there at the top of the pass ... and there it was, stretching away from the foot of the mountain, the great pan of the Karoo ... stretching away forever, it seemed, into the purple haze and heat of the horizon. Something grabbed my heart at that moment, my soul, and squeezed it until there were tears in my eyes. I had never seen anything so big, so beautiful in all my life. I went to the teacher who was with us and asked him: "Teacher, where will I come to if I start walking that way" ... and I pointed. He laughed. "Little man, " he said, "that way is north. If you start walking that way and just keep on walking, and your legs don't give in, you will see all of Africa! Yes, Africa, little man! You will see the great rivers of the continent: the Vaal, the Zambesi, the Limpopo, the Congo and then the mighty Nile. You will see the mountains: the Drakensberg, Kilimanjaro, Kenya and the Ruwenzori. And you will meet all our brothers: the little Pygmies of the forests, the proud Masai, the Watusi ... tallest of the tall and the Kikuyu standing on one leg like herons in a pond waiting for a frog." "Has teacher seen all that?" I asked. "No," he said. "Then how does teacher know it's there?" "Because it is all in the books and I have read the books and if you work hard in school, little man, you can do the same without worrying about your legs giving in."

He was right, Thami. *I* have seen it. It is all there in the books just as he said it was and I have made it mine. I can stand on the banks of all those great rivers, look up at the majesty of all those mountains, whenever I want to. It is a journey I have made many times, Whenever my spirit was low and I sat alone in my room, I said to myself: Walk, Anela! Walk! ... and I imagined myself at the foot of the Wapadsberg setting off for that horizon that called me that day forty years ago. It always worked! When I left that little room, I walked back into the world a proud man, because I was an African and all the splendor was my birthright.

(*Pause.*) I don't want to make that journey again, Thami. There is someone waiting for me now at the end of it who has made a mockery of all my visions of splendor. He has in his arms my real birthright. I saw him on the television in the Reverend Mbop's lounge. An Ethiopian tribesman, and he was carrying the body of a little child that had died of hunger in the famine ... a small bundle carelessly wrapped in a few rags. I couldn't tell how old the man was. The lines of despair and starvation on his face made him look as old as Africa itself.

He held that little bundle very lightly as he shuffled along to a mass grave, and when he reached it, he didn't have the strength to kneel and lay it down gently ... He just opened his arms and let it fall. I was very upset when the program ended. Nobody had thought to tell us his name and whether he was the child's father, or grandfather, or uncle. And the same for the baby! Didn't it have a name? How dare you show me one of our children being thrown away and not tell me its name! I demand to know who is in that bundle!

(*Pause.*) Not knowing their names doesn't matter anymore. They are more than just themselves. The tribesmen and dead child do duty for all of us, Thami. Every African soul is either carrying that bundle or in it.

What is wrong with this world that it wants to waste you all like that ... my children ... my Africa! (*Holding out a hand as if he wanted to touch Thami's face.*) My beautiful and proud young Africa!

(*More BREAKING GLASS and stones and the SOUND of a crowd outside the school. MR. M starts to move. THAMI stops him.*)

THAMI. No! Don't go out there. Let me speak to them first. Listen to me! I will tell them I have confronted you with the charges and that you have denied them and that I believe you. I will tell them you are innocent.

MR. M. You will lie for me, Thami?

THAMI. Yes.

MR. M. (*Desperate to hear the truth.*) Why?

(*THAMI can't speak.*)

MR. M. Why will you lie for me, Thami?

THAMI. I've told you before.

MR. M. The "Cause?"

THAMI. Yes.

MR. M. Then I do not need to hide behind your lies.

THAMI. They will kill you.

MR. M. Do you think I'm frightened of them? Do you think I'm frightened of dying? (*MR. M breaks away from Thami. Ringing his bell furiously HE goes outside and confronts the mob. THEY kill him.*)

Scene 4

THAMI waiting. ISABEL arrives.

THAMI. Isabel.

ISABEL. (*It takes her a few seconds to respond.*) Hello, Thami.

THAMI. Thank you for coming.

ISABEL. (*SHE is tense. Talking to him is not easy.*) I wasn't going to. Let me tell you straight out that there is nothing in this world ... nothing! ... that I want to see less at this moment than anything or anybody from the location. But you said in your note that it was urgent, so here I am. If you've got something to say, I'll listen.

THAMI. Are you in a hurry?

ISABEL. I haven't got to be somewhere else, if that's what you mean. But if you're asking because it looks as if I would like to run away from here, from you! ... very fast, then the answer is yes. But don't worry, I'll be able to control that urge for as long as you need to say what you want to.

THAMI. (*Awkward in the face of Isabel's severe and unyielding attitude.*) I just wanted to say goodbye.

ISABEL. Again?

THAMI. What do you mean?

ISABEL. You've already done that, Thami. Maybe you didn't use that word, but you turned your back on me and walked out of my life that last afternoon the three of us ... (*SHE can't finish.*) How long ago was that?

THAMI. Three weeks I think.

ISABEL. So why do you want to do it again? Aren't you happy with the last time? It was so dramatic, Thami.

THAMI. (*Patiently.*) I wanted to see you because I'm leaving the town, I'm going away for good.

ISABEL. Oh, I see. This is meant to be a "sad" goodbye is it? (*SHE is on the edge.*) I'm sorry if I'm hurting your feelings but I thought you wanted to see me because you had something to say about recent events in our little community ... (*Out of a pocket a crumpled little piece of newspaper which SHE opens with unsteady hands.*) ... a certain unrest related ... I think that is the phrase they use ... yes ... here it is .... (*Reading.*) "... unrest related incident in which according to witnesses the defenseless teacher was attacked by a group of blacks who struck him over the head with an iron rod before setting him on fire."

THAMI. Stop it, Isabel.

ISABEL. (*Fighting hard for self-control.*) Oh, Thami I wish I could! I've tried everything, but nothing helps. It just keeps going around and around inside my head. I've tried crying. I've tried praying! I've even tried confrontation. Ja, the day after it happened I tried to get into the location. I wanted to find the witnesses who reported it so accurately and ask them: ... why didn't you stop it! There was a police roadblock at the entrance and they wouldn't let me in. They thought I was crazy or something and "escorted" me back into the safekeeping of two now very frightened parents.

There is nothing wrong with me! All I need is someone to tell me why he was killed. What madness drove those people to kill a man who had devoted his whole life to helping them. He was such a good man, Thami! He was one of the most beautiful human beings I have ever known and his death is the ugliest thing I have ever known.

THAMI. (*Gives her a few seconds to calm down. Gently.*) He was an informer, Isabel. Somehow or the other somebody discovered that Mr. M was an informer.

ISABEL. You mean that list of pupils taking part in the boycott? You call that informing?

THAMI. No. It was worse than that. He went to the police and gave them the names and addresses of our political action committee. All of them were arrested after his visit. They are now in detention.

ISABEL. Mr. M did that?

THAMI. Yes.

ISABEL. I don't believe it.

THAMI. It's true, Isabel.

ISABEL. No! What proof do you have?

THAMI. His own words. He told me so himself. I didn't believe it either when he was first accused, but the last time I saw him, he said it was true, that he had been to the police.

ISABEL. (*Stunned disbelief.*) Mr. M? A police spy? For how long?

THAMI. No. It wasn't like that. He wasn't paid or anything. He went to the police just that one time. He said he felt it was his duty.

ISABEL. What do you mean?

THAMI. Operation Qhumisa ... the boycotts and strikes, the arson ... you know he didn't agree with any of that. But he was also very confused about it all. I think he wished he had never done it.

ISABEL. So he went to the police just once.

THAMI. Yes.

ISABEL. As a matter of conscience.

THAMI. Yes.

ISABEL. That doesn't make him an "informer," Thami!

THAMI. Then what do you call somebody who gives information to the police?

ISABEL. No! You know what that word really means, the sort of person it suggests. Was Mr. M one of those? He was acting out of concern for his people ... you said so yourself. He thought he was doing the right thing! You don't murder a man for that!

THAMI. (*Near the end of his patience.*) Be careful, Isabel.

ISABEL. Of what?

THAMI. The words you use.

ISABEL. Oh? Which one don't you like? Murder? What do you want me to call it ... "an unrest related incident?" If you are going to call him an informer, then I am going to call his death murder!

THAMI. It was an act of self-defense.

ISABEL. By who?

THAMI. The People.

ISABEL. (*Almost speechless with outrage.*) What? A mad mob attacks one unarmed defenseless man and you want me to call it ...

THAMI. (*Abandoning all attempts at patience. HE speaks with the full authority of the anger inside him.*) Stop it, Isabel! You just keep quiet now and listen to me. You're always saying you want to understand us and what it means to be black ... well if you do, listen to me carefully now. I don't call it murder, and I don't call the people who did it a mad mob and yes, I do expect you to see it as an act of self-defense ... listen to me! ... blind and stupid but still self-defense.

He betrayed us and our fight for freedom. Five men are in detention because of Mr. M's visit to the police station. There have been other arrests and there will be more. Why do you think I'm running away?

How were those people to know he wasn't a paid informer who had been doing it for a long time and would do it again? They were defending themselves against what they thought was a terrible danger to themselves. What Anela Myalatya did to them and their cause is what your laws define as treason when it is done to you and threatens the safety and security of your comfortable white world. Anybody accused of it is put on trial in your courts and if found guilty they get hanged. Many of my people have been found guilty and have been hanged. Those hangings *we* call murder!

Try to understand, Isabel. Try to imagine what it is like to be a black person, choking inside with rage and frustration, bitterness, and then to discover that one of your own kind is a traitor, has betrayed you to those responsible for the suffering and misery of your family, of your people. What would you do? Remember there is no magistrate or court you can drag him to and demand that he be tried for that crime. There is no justice for black people in this country other than what we make for ourselves. When you judge us for what happened in front of the school four days ago just remember that you carry a share of the responsibility for it. It is your laws that have made simple, decent black people so desperate that they turn into "mad mobs."

(*ISABEL has been listening and watching intently. It looks as if SHE is going to say something but SHE stops herself.*)

THAMI. Say it, Isabel.
ISABEL. No.
THAMI. This is your last chance. You once challenged me to be honest with you. I'm challenging you now.
ISABEL. (*SHE faces him.*) Where were you when it happened, Thami? (*Pause.*) And if you were, did you try to stop them?
THAMI. Isn't there a third question, Isabel? Was I one of the mob that killed him?
ISABEL. Yes. Forgive me, Thami ... please forgive me! ...But there is that question as well. Only once! Believe me, only once ... late at night when I couldn't sleep. I couldn't believe it was there in my head, but I

heard the words ... "Was Thami one of the ones who did it?"

THAMI. If the police catch me, that's the question they will ask.

ISABEL. I'm asking you because ... (*An open, helpless gesture.*) ... I'm lost! I don't know what to think or feel anymore. Help me. Please. You're the only one who can. Nobody else seems to understand that I loved him. (*This final confrontation is steady and unflinching on both sides.*)

THAMI. Yes, I was there. Yes, I did try to stop it. (*THAMI gives Isabel the time to deal with his answer.*) I knew how angry the people were. I went to warn him. If he had listened to me he would still be alive, but he wouldn't. It was almost as if he wanted it to happen. I think he hated himself very much for what he had done, Isabel. He kept saying to me that it was all over. He was right. There was nothing left for him. That visit to the police station had finished everything. Nobody would have ever spoken to him again or let him teach their children.

ISABEL. Oh, Thami, it is all so wrong! So stupid! That's what I can't take ... the terrible stupidity of it. We needed him. All of us.

THAMI. I know.

ISABEL. Then why is he dead?

THAMI. You must stop asking these questions, Isabel. You know the answers.

ISABEL. They don't make any sense, Thami.

THAMI. I know what you are feeling. (*Pause.*) I also loved him. Doesn't help much to say it now, I know, but I did. Because he made me angry and impatient with his "old-fashioned" ideas, I didn't want to admit it. Even if I had, it wouldn't have stopped me from doing what I did, the boycott and everything, but I should have tried harder to make him understand why I was doing it. You were right to ask about that. Now ...? (*A helpless gesture.*) You know the most terrible words in your language, Isabel? Too late.

ISABEL. Ja.

THAMI. I'll never forgive myself for not trying harder with him and letting him know ... my true feelings for him. Right until the end I tried to deny it ... to him, to myself.

ISABEL. I'm sorry. I ...

THAMI. That's all right.

ISABEL. Are the police really looking for you?

THAMI. Yes. Some of my friends have already been detained. They're pulling in anybody they can get their hands on.

ISABEL. Where are you going? Cape Town?

THAMI. No. That's the first place they'll look. I've written to my parents telling them about everything. I'm heading north.

ISABEL. To where?

THAMI. Far, Isabel. I'm leaving the country.

ISABEL. Does that mean what I think it does?

THAMI. (*Nods.*) I'm going to join the movement. I want to be a fighter. I've been thinking about it for a long time. Now I know it's the right thing to do. I don't want to end up being one of the mob that killed Mr. M—but that will happen to me if I stay here.

ISABEL. Oh, Thami.

THAMI. I know I'm doing the right thing. Believe me.

ISABEL. I'll try.

THAMI. And you?

ISABEL. I don't know what to do with myself, Thami. All I know is that I'm frightened of losing him. He's only been dead four days and I think I'm already starting to forget what he looked like. But the worst thing is that there's nowhere for me to go and ... you know ... just be near him. That's so awful. I got my father to phone the police but they said there wasn't enough left of him to justify a grave. What there was had been disposed of in a "Christian manner." So where do I go? The burnt-out ruins of the school? I couldn't face that.

THAMI. Get you father or somebody to drive you to the top of the Wapadsberg Pass. It's on the road to Craddock.

ISABEL. I know it.

THAMI. It was a very special place to him. He told me that it was there where it all started, where he knew what he wanted to do with his life ... being a teacher, being the Mr. M we knew. You'll be near him up there. I must go now.

ISABEL. Do you need any money?

THAMI. No. Sala Kakuhle, Isabel. That's the Xhosa goodbye.

ISABEL. I know it. Asispumla taught me how to say it. Hamba Kakhule, Thami.

(*THAMI leaves.*)

Scene 5

ISABEL. (*Alone. SHE stands quietly, examining the silence. After a few seconds SHE nods her head slowly.*) Yes! Thami was right, Mr. M. He said I'd feel near you up here.

He's out there somewhere, Mr. M ... travelling north. He didn't say where exactly he was going, but I think we can guess, can't we?

I'm here for a very "old-fashioned" reason, so I know you'll approve. I've come to pay my last respects to Anela Myalatya. I know the old-fashioned way of doing that is to

bring flowers, lay them on the grave, say a quiet prayer and
then go back to your life. But that seemed sort of silly this
time. You'll have enough flowers around here when the
spring comes ... which it will. So instead I've brought you
something which I know will mean more to you than
flowers or prayers ever could. A promise. I am going to
make Anela Myalatya a promise.

You gave me a little lecture once about wasted lives ...
how much of it you'd seen, how much you hated it, how
much you didn't want that to happen to Thami and me. I
sort of understood what you meant at the time. Now, I
most certainly do. Your death has seen to that.

My promise to you is that I am going to try as hard as I
can, in every way that I can, to see that it doesn't happen
to me. I am going to try my best to make my life useful in
the way yours was. I want you to be proud of me. After
all, I am one of your children you know. You did welcome
me to your family. (*A pause.*) The future is still ours, Mr.
M. (*The ACTRESS leaves the stage.*)

The End

COSTUME PLOT

ISABEL
I:1
Gym (blue)
Blouse (white)
Tie (striped)
Blazer (blue striped)
Hat (straw boater)
Knee socks (gray with blue stripe)
Panties (blue)
Shoes (black)
I:2
Same (without boater)
I:3
Same as I:2
I:4
Blouse (same)
Skirt (blue)
Sweater (white)
Scarf
Socks (white with gold and blue stripe)
Hockey boots
Panties (same)
II:1
Blouse (same)
Gym (same)
Panties (same)
Sweater (blue cardigan)
Bare feet
II:4
Sweater (white wool)
Sweatpants (gray)
Jacket (blue)
Scarf (gray)

Socks
Sneakers
II:5
Same as II:4

Watch throughout

MR. M
Shirt (white)
Suit (tan)
Tie
Vest (gray knit)
Socks (gray)
Shoes (brown)
Hat (fedora gray)
Watch
Undershirt (white)

THAMI
I:1
Shirt (white)
Tie (striped)
Sweater (maroon)
Pants (gray wool)
Socks (black)
Shoes (black tie)

I:4
Same as I:1 without tie
II:1
Shirt (blue)
Pants (same)
Shoes (same)
Socks (same)

II:3
T-shirt (tan)
Jeans
Sweatshirt (brown with zipped front)
Socks (black)
Sneakers (black)
II:4
Same as II:3

Watch throughout

PROPERTY PLOT

<u>SET</u>
Desk, Desk chair, 2 Chairs, Bench, Blackboard, Upholstered Chair, Small Oriental Carpet, Rock, Chalk and Eraser

<u>HAND PROPS</u>

Mr. M: School Bell, Dictionary, Matchbox, Roll Book, Exercise Books, Assorted Pens, Briefcase, Program, Written Proposal

ISABEL: Satchel, Assorted School Books, Assorted Notebooks, Assorted Pens & Pencils, Debate Speech, Hockey Stick, Gear Bag, Newspaper Article, 3 Sets Typed Bios

THAMI: Knapsack, Handwritten Debate Speech, Notepad, Pencil, Coin

The Classroom, Act One Scene i
Act Two Scene iii

Curtain open

Chalkboard and easel

Table and 3 straight wooden chairs

A} Two poles with
B} curtain - wire and
2 foot high curtain

Bench (Thami's desk)

Level B.g.

Level Flr

ACT ONE   Scenes iii and v

Curtain closed.

Bench position for Scene iii

Bench position for Scene v

Act Two Scene i

Carpet and
Plush chair

Also By

Athol Fugard

BLOOD KNOT

BOESMAN AND LENA

THE ISLAND

A LESSON FROM ALOES

MASTER HAROLD...AND THE BOYS

HELLO AND GOODBYE

THE ROAD TO MECCA

PEOPLE ARE LIVING THERE

SIZWE BANZI IS DEAD

STATEMENTS AFTER AN ARREST
UNDER THE IMMORALITY ACT

OTHER TITLES AVAILABLE FROM SAMUEL FRENCH

JITNEY
August Wilson

Drama / 8m, 1f / Interiors
Set in 1970 in the Hill District of Pittsburgh that is served by
a makeshift taxi company, Jitney is a beautiful addition to
the author's decade by decade cycle of plays about the black
American experience in the twentieth century.

"Could be described as just a lot of men sitting around
talking. But the talk has such varied range and musicality, and
it is rendered with such stylish detail, that a complete urban
symphony emerges.... Drivers return from jobs with stories
that summon an entire ethos.... Throughly engrossing, *Jitney*
holds us in charmed captivity."
– *New York Times*

"Explosive... Crackles with theatrical energy."
– *New York Daily News*

Award Winning!
New York Drama Critics Award for Best New Play
Outer Critics Circle Award for Outstanding Off Broadway Play

OTHER TITLES AVAILABLE FROM SAMUEL FRENCH

OUTRAGE
Itamar Moses

Drama / 8m, 2f / Unit Set

In Ancient Greece, Socrates is accused of corrupting the young with his practice of questioning commonly held beliefs. In Renaissance Italy, a simple miller named Menocchio runs afoul of the Inquisition when he develops his own theory of the cosmos. In Nazi Germany, the playwright Bertolt Brecht is persecuted for work that challenges authority. And in present day New England, a graduate student finds himself in the center of a power struggle over the future of the University. An irreverent epic that spans thousands of years, *Outrage* explores the power of martyrdom, the power of theatre, and how the revolutionary of one era become the tyrant of the next.

THE HOUSE OF BLUE LEAVES
John Guare

Farce / 4m, 6f / Interior

Artie Shaugnessy is a songwriter with visions of glory. Toiling by day as a zoo-keeper, he suffers in seedy lounges by night, plying his wares at piano bars in Queens, New York where he lives with his wife, Bananas. Artie's downstairs mistress, Bunny Flingus will sleep with him anytime but refuses to cook until they are married. On the day the Pope is making his first visit to the city, Artie's son Ronny goes AWOL from Fort Dix stowing a home made-bomb intended to blow up the Pope in Yankee Stadium. Also arriving is Artie's old school chum, now a successful Hollywood producer, Billy Einhorn with starlet girlfriend in tow, who holds the key to Artie's dreams of getting out of Queens and away from the life he so despises. But like many dreams, this promise of glory evaporates amid the chaos of ordinary lives.

"Enchantingly zany and original farce."
– *The New York Times*

SAMUEL FRENCH STAFF

Nate Collins
President

Ken Dingledine
Director of Operations,
Vice President

Bruce Lazarus
Executive Director

Rita Maté
Director of Finance

ACCOUNTING

Lori Thimsen | Director of Licensing Compliance
Nehal Kumar | Senior Accounting Associate
Josephine Messina | Accounts Payable
Helena Mezzina | Royalty Administration
Joe Garner | Royalty Administration
Jessica Zheng | Accounts Receivable
Andy Lian | Accounts Receivable
Zoe Qiu | Accounts Receivable
Charlie Sou | Accounting Associate
Joann Mannello | Orders Administrator

BUSINESS AFFAIRS

Lysna Marzani | Director of Business Affairs
Kathryn McCumber | Business Administrator

CUSTOMER SERVICE AND LICENSING

Brad Lohrenz | Director of Licensing Development
Billie Davis | Licensing Service Manager
Fred Schnitzer | Business Development Manager
Melody Fernandez | Amateur Licensing Supervisor
Laura Lindson | Professional Licensing Supervisor
John Tracey | Professional Licensing Associate
Kim Rogers | Amateur Licensing Associate
Matthew Akers | Amateur Licensing Associate
Jay Clark | Amateur Licensing Associate
Alicia Grey | Amateur Licensing Associate
Ashley Byrne | Amateur Licensing Associate
Jake Glickman | Amateur Licensing Associate
Chris Lonstrup | Amateur Licensing Associate
Jabez Zuniga | Amateur Licensing Associate
Glenn Halcomb | Amateur Licensing Associate
Derek Hassler | Amateur Licensing Associate
Jennifer Carter | Amateur Licensing Associate

EDITORIAL AND PUBLICATIONS

Amy Rose Marsh | Literary Manager
Ben Coleman | Editorial Associate
Gene Sweeney | Graphic Designer
David Geer | Publications Supervisor
Charlyn Brea | Publications Associate
Tyler Mullen | Publications Associate

MARKETING

Abbie Van Nostrand | Director of Marketing
Alison Sundstrom | Marketing Associate

OPERATIONS

Joe Ferreira | Product Development Manager
Casey McLain | Operations Supervisor
Danielle Heckman | Office Coordinator, Reception

SAMUEL FRENCH BOOKSHOP (LOS ANGELES)

Joyce Mehess | Bookstore Manager
Cory DeLair | Bookstore Buyer
Jennifer Palumbo | Customer Service Associate
Sonya Wallace | Bookstore Associate
Tim Coultas | Bookstore Associate
Monté Patterson | Bookstore Associate
Robin Hushbeck | Bookstore Associate
Alfred Contreras | Shipping & Receiving

LONDON OFFICE

Felicity Barks | Submissions Associate
Steve Blacker | Bookshop Associate
David Bray | Customer Services Associate
Zena Choi | Professional Licensing Associate
Robert Cooke | Assistant Buyer
Stephanie Dawson | Amateur Licensing Associate
Simon Ellison | Retail Sales Manager
Jason Felix | Royalty Administration
Susan Griffiths | Amateur Licensing Associate
Robert Hamilton | Amateur Licensing Associate
Lucy Hume | Publications Associate
Nasir Khan | Management Accountant
Simon Magniti | Royalty Administration
Louise Mappley | Amateur Licensing Associate
James Nicolau | Despatch Associate
Martin Phillips | Librarian
Zubayed Rahman | Despatch Associate
Steve sanderson | Royalty Administration Supervisor
Roger Sheppard | I.T. Manager
Geoffrey Skinner | Company Accountant
Peter Smith | Amateur Licensing Associate
Garry Spratley | Customer Service Manager
David Webster | UK Operations Director

SAMUELFRENCH.COM
SAMUELFRENCH-LONDON.CO.UK